HOW YOU CAN

BE PREPARED

By Jim McKeever

HOW YOU CAN BE PREPARED

Copyright © 1980 by James M. McKeever

Omega Publications
P.O. Box 4130
Medford, Oregon 97501

ISBN 0-931608-12-0 (Hardbound)
ISBN 0-931608-13-9 (Softbound)

TABLE OF CONTENTS

1

Be Prepared for

THIS BOOK

When I was in the Boy Scouts, our motto was, "Be Prepared." I certainly appreciate all the valuable training our leaders gave us. We learned not only how to find our way out of the woods when lost, but also how to survive in the woods in the event that we had to. We were taught how to start a fire without using matches, how to build a lean-to out of tree limbs, how to find and cook wild edible foods, and many other skills for surviving such an experience.

As a consulting economist, I have often thought that someone should prepare a "Be Prepared" manual to help those who are lost in the jungle of our nightmarish economic and financial world. Just as some of the knowledge a Boy Scout gains can actually save his life, so some of the knowledge you might gain from this book could save your financial life and possibly even your physical life.

Financially, we are all living in an extremely unstable
and increasingly chaotic economy. As we begin to see
our standard of living gradually slip out from under
us and we look from astronomical inflation rates to
Mid-East oil cartels to determine where our next
economic flak will come from, we must wonder if we
shouldn't be doing something now to prepare for severe
economic problems in the future.

Thinking in terms of sheer physical survival, you'll
have to agree that our world today is becoming progressively more violent. Terrorism is becoming more
widespread throughout the world. We can easily imagine even here in America violence more widespread
and massive than what we saw in Watts and Los Angeles
in the 1970's or, more recently, in Miami in the 1980's.

It's important that we think through the possibilities
for both our economic and physical future and make
preparation for whatever we feel lies ahead. This
book is written on how to be prepared for the future
as I perceive it.

IT IS IMPORTANT THAT YOU REALIZE that, for the most
part, these chapters were articles taken directly from
my newsletter, *The McKeever Strategy Letter (MSL)*.
These articles have not been changed at all, so we ask
that you ignore those references that pertained at the
time of the writing but are not presently applicable.
If you will kindly read around these, we feel you will
find information and insights highly valuable to your
efforts at becoming prepared for the future.

As you will see as you begin to read this book, it is
based on the scenario that we are going to have more
and even worse inflation in the United States across
the next ten to twenty years. We realize that there
is a debate going on over whether we are facing more
inflation or a deflation. We are firmly on the inflation side of this debate, and the early chapters
give our reasons for this.

THE SINGLE MOST IMPORTANT INVESTMENT DECISION A PERSON WILL MAKE IN THE 1980'S IS ON THE INFLATION VS. DEFLATION QUESTION.

Many people who attend monetary conferences and read investment newsletters are vacillating between these two positions. My advice is to get off the fence and move into one camp or the other because the strategies to prepare for each are very different. We believe that one should prepare for more and worse inflation.

You should not be confused by the assumption that inflation and depression are opposites. They are not. Inflation and deflation are opposites, and depression and business boom are opposites. In the early 1920's, Germany experienced a depression and simultaneously a runaway inflation. This was an inflationary-depression. During the early 1930's the United States experienced a depression with prices dropping. This was a deflationary-depression.

I believe we are going to have a depression, but that it will be of the inflationary type. Most people wrongly assume that if we have a depression it will be of the deflationary type that we experienced earlier in this century. In a later chapter we will discuss this inflationary type of depression in detail and provide some thoughts on how you can prepare for it.

So let's begin by taking a look at how to prepare for the inflation that will change your life.

2

Be Prepared for
WORSE INFLATION

Reprinted from MISL #184, April 1979

These two questions have to be burning in the mind of
every thinking individual who is concerned about the
financial future of his family. With inflation running
at 12%-15%, even by conservative government figures,
everyone's financial life will be affected, either for
the better or for the worse. (Yes, there *is* a way inflation can affect your financial life for the better!
We'll talk about that later in this article.) First
let's turn to these two fundamental questions.

MCKEEVER'S RULE #1 FOR THE 1980'S:

INFLATION WILL CONTINUE AND WORSEN

The longtime readers of MISL all understand what inflation is, and what causes it. But because of a whole
host of new subscribers, we need to say a few words
about inflation itself, to lay the foundation for rule
#1. (I hope our faithful readers will forgive this re-
petition. However, even for you it might not hurt to
review my thinking on this subject.)

To an economist, the definition of inflation is very
clean and simple: it is the increase in the money supply over and above the increase in productivity. Since
that is not the way the word "inflation" is normally
used, this increase is the money supply we will call true
inflation, or monetary inflation. In this article we
will use the bare term "inflation" to refer to the rise
in the prices of goods and services. According to Web-
ster's, inflation is "expansion due to the injection of hot
air or gas." This is what the government is doing to our
money supply. Monetary inflation causes (price) inflation.

In order to help you understand why this is true, I would
like to use my familiar (and famous?) illustration. If
there were a group of people assembled in your living
room and I passed out Monopoly money to them and held an
auction of the items in the room (pictures, lamps,
tables, chairs, vases, etc.) we would come up with one
level of prices. However, if we had the same group of
people in the same living room and I passed out twice as
much Monopoly money and held the same auction, what would
happen to the prices? The answer that is they would double. The passing out of additional money (monetary inflation) *causes* prices to rise (inflation). It's as
simple as that.

When you read that the government is deficit spending by
$30 billion, by and large they are creating 30 billion
extra dollars and passing them out. As these additional
dollars flow through the economy, the prices will rise
proportionally. This is why those who understand are
now clamoring for a balanced federal budget. They think
that it will bring inflation under control. It would
certainly help, if a law were passed and implemented.
However, as we pointed out in recent issues, there are
a number of ways - off-budget deficits, fractional banking ratios, and guaranteed loans - that the government
can continue to create this money without deficit spending. I believe that with or without a Constitutional
Amendment, we will continue to have deficit spending in
the federal government.

There are a number of reasons for this. One is that the beneficiaries now outnumber the producers. (Remember, the beneficiaries include all government workers, the military, subsidized farmers, welfare recipients, social security recipients, and the list goes on and on). As long as the beneficiaries can vote, they will vote themselves a bigger and bigger share of the national pie.

Another reason that I believe inflation will continue we have covered many times before, and that is that our elected representatives like to play Santa Claus. When special interest groups come to them with requests, they like to hand out the goodies so that they can get re-elected. Rather than being statesmen, and raising taxes to cover the additional expenditures, most elected re-presentatives would by far rather inflate the money sup-ply.

Let's summarize what we are saying. I believe that in-flation is going to continue because of some basic low moral and ethical values that exist in the United States. The work ethic is gone. We give incentives to people not to work. Our elected representatives really don't represent us. The beneficiaries outnumber the producers. There is no gold backing for our currency, and every fiat (unbacked) currency in history has ultimately become worthless. You can believe the deflationists' scenario if you want to, but my clear statement and warning to one and all is to get prepared for bigger and worse in-flation. To be sure, there will be ups and downs in the inflation rate, but as we look at the 1980's, the trend is up, up and maybe away.

WILL INFLATION GET OUT OF CONTROL?

The answer to this question is not nearly so clear. There are many other alternatives as to what could hap-pen. One thing that could happen is that we could have total wage and price controls (remember, I am still pro-jecting those for later in this year). This means we could eventually go into primarily a totally controlled economy, much like Russia's. Another alternative is that we could go the route of any of the Latin American countries and rock along with 100%-360% inflation per year. (I call this hyperinflation.) Some of these Latin American countries have been doing this for many years, without *runaway* inflation occurring.

The third possibility would be that we could get into a runaway inflation. I would not consider inflation to be out of control (runaway) until prices were escalating more than 1% per day (360% per year). At that point in time, there would probably be an inflationary blow off, with money becoming worthless quickly. I believe we are quite a ways from this, and that we would have plenty of warning in order to change our strategy to prepare for runaway inflation.

Now we need to be concerned about regular inflation (10%-29% per year), severe inflation (30%-99% per year), and hyperinflation (100%-360% per year). We need to look at ways of how to protect ourselves, and even benefit from inflation.

MCKEEVER'S RULE #2 FOR THE 1980'S:

> *WEALTH WILL BE TRANSFERRED*
> *FROM LENDERS TO BORROWERS*

Inflation causes wealth to be transferred. By "wealth", we are talking about purchasing power. Now let's look at *how* inflation transfers wealth from the lenders to the borrowers.

We will use a simple example of three men. The table below shows their financial status now, and what happens to their financial status after prices of everything (including their houses) double. Neil Neutral had a $10,000 loan against his house and $10,000 in a savings account. In reality, this $10,000 in a savings account says that he has loaned this amount to a local Savings and Loan association. The amount of money that he owes and the amount of money owed to him are the same. His lending/borrowing ratio is 1/1, which is 1.00. This puts him in a neutral position. Thus, if the price of his house doubles, his net worth will also exactly double. This means

13

that his net worth has the same amount of purchasing power as it did before the prices of everything, including his house, doubled.

NEIL NEUTRAL (1/1 = 1.00)	NOW	WHEN PRICES DOUBLE
ASSETS		
Savings (Lending)	$ 10,000	$ 10,000
House	80,000	160,000
LIABILITIES AND NET WORTH		
Loan (Borrowing)	10,000	10,000
Net Worth	80,000	160,000
BENNY BORROWER (1/6 = 0.17)		
ASSETS		
Savings (Lending)	$ 10,000	$ 10,000
House	80,000	160,000
LIABILITIES AND NET WORTH		
Loan (Borrowing)	60,000	60,000
Net Worth	30,000	110,000
LARRY LENDER (8/1 = 8.00)		
ASSETS		
Savings (Lending)	$ 80,000	$ 80,000
House	80,000	160,000
LIABILITIES AND NET WORTH		
Loan (Borrowing)	10,000	10,000
Net Worth	150,000	230,000

Benny Borrower has a $60,000 loan against his house and his lending/borrowing ratio is 1/6, or 0.17. He is in good shape to take advantage of the transfer of wealth by inflation. His net worth starts out at $30,000, but after the price of everything doubles, his net worth is $110,000. This is an increase in net worth of almost 4 times, while prices only doubled. Therefore, his real purchasing power has almost doubled.

Larry Lender is exactly the opposite. He has just about

paid off his house, and has a large amount of money in a savings account. His lending/borrowing ratio is 8/1, which is equal to 8.00. He is in bad shape as far as inflation goes. When the prices of everything double, his net worth does not even *double*; it only goes from $150,000 to $230,000. It needed to go to at least $300,000 for him to simply break even. His net worth only increased 44% while prices increased 100%. Thus, Larry Lender *lost* wealth because of inflation, while Benny Borrower gained net worth because of inflation.

First let me point out that what we have labeled as "savings" is really anything measured in a fixed amount of paper dollars. This could be a mortgage you took back when you sold a piece of property, a whole life insurance policy, bonds, a retirement policy, money you loaned to relatives, friends or your own company. Under the category "loan", this could be a mortgage against your house, money borrowed for an investment in a farm, personal loans, credit cards and so forth.

I would encourage each of our readers to sit down and calculate his own personal lending/borrowing ratio. If it is above 1.00, inflation will steal wealth from you. The bigger the number, the worse you will fare in inflation. In this case (just like in golf scores), the smaller the number, the better. Therefore, if your number is below 0.4 you should be set alright for inflation. Before you erroneously charge out and recklessly borrow money, or run up credit card bills, we need to take a look at credit.

WISE USE OF CREDIT

A general rule of thumb is that an individual, at any one point in time, should owe approximately 5 times his annual salary. This means that if your annual salary is $30,000, you should right now have borrowed approximately $150,000. If you find yourself falling far short of this, or with a lending/borrowing ratio greater than 1, you may wish to intelligently borrow some money for investment purposes. In the next issue, we will be looking in detail at areas in which these funds could be placed. A simple example is that one could go buy a

rural piece of property worth $100,000. By making a
$20,000-$30,000 down payment, the owner frequently will
carry the "paper", and thus you will fairly easily improve your ratio (since you will have just borrowed
$70,000-$80,000).

Another area that we should look to for increasing our
borrowing, where we already have approved credit, is
through our credit cards. Most people use credit cards
in a very stupid way. (If I offend you, I'm glad. Perhaps it will jolt you into wise use of credit cards.)
Credit cards can either give you a continual 30-day, in-
terest-free loan or they can eat you alive, forcing you
to pay a ridiculous 18% interest. Credit cards used
properly must be paid in full *every time* you receive a
bill, and never, *never* any interest paid on them. If
you cannot use credit cards this way, my advise would
be take out the scissors, cut them in half and throw
them away. Even if you have to borrow the money to
initially pay them off, you would be paying less interest than you would be paying to the credit card companies. I would do it and then discipline myself to
every month totally pay off the credit card. If for
any reason some month you were not able to do this,
I would lock that credit card away somewhere and not
use it again until it was paid off completely.

It is just interesting to note that, from my best financial information, Sears & Roebuck basically breaks
even on the merchandise they sell. Almost *all* of their
profit comes from the interest payments that their credit
card customers pay to them. Therefore, companies like
Sears will do everything they can to encourage you to
charge and to charge more.

This paying off of credit cards goes for any department
store or gasoline company, as well as VISA (Master Charge
is now owned by VISA), American Express, and so forth.
If you can't pay them off *every month*, destroy them.

HOW TO BORROW ON YOUR HOME EQUITY

For many people, the big investment is their home, and
to improve their lending/borrowing ratio, they would
likely have to borrow money against their home equity.

Personal Finance (P.O. Box 2599, Landover Hills, MD 20784), in the December 20, 1978 issue, had an excellent write-up on this subject. They said:

"The best investment most people have made in recent years is their home. But how do you capitalize on that appreciation when you need the money for, say, invest-ment purposes, a second home, or to pay off pressing debts? Most people are apparently cashing in on the equity in their homes by refinancing their mortgages, which isn't always a wise idea. In many cases, a second mortgage may end up being a lot cheaper than refinancing your original mortgage.

"To begin with, you'll save substantial paperwork and legal fees by getting a second mortgage. When you re-finance, you usually have to go through the whole busi-ness of closing again. That means pretty hefty costs - just to get a new mortgage drawn up can cost you $2,000. And if there's a prepayment clause, you may also have to pay what could be a substantial sum as a penalty for prepaying your original mortgage.

"By contrast, second mortgages don't disturb your orig-inal mortgage - which means you won't have to pay new closing costs or a penalty fee. The only fee you'll probably have to pay is a one-time charge that ranges from $15 to $150 to cover the paperwork. One of the reasons why the costs are low is that the lender is con-cerned mainly with your ability to meet the payments, and hence won't spend considerable sums analyzing the value of the property.

"And even the interest rates on a second mortgage - which range anywhere from 11.5 to 18 percent - may not be as bad as they seem at first glance. That's espe-cially true if you recently took out a first mortgage and haven't yet made much of a dent in the principal re-payments. In fact, refinancing your original mortgage would probably be cheaper only if you have paid it down to the point where you have considerably reduced the amount of principal that you owe - which usually takes over 10 years. (A typical mortgage is structured so that the early payments - say, for the first 10 years -

are heavily weighted toward the interest. If you refinanced, you'd have to start paying interest on the
amount now outstanding as well as the additional money
you borrow. Over the long-term, that could be costlier
than a second mortgage.)

"Here's how the numbers look: Let's assume that you
bought your home 10 years ago for $55,000. Let's say
you took out a 25-year mortgage for 90 percent of the
value of the house, or $50,000, at an interest rate of
6½ percent. Now assume that 10 years later your house
has appreciated at an annual rate of 3 percent (a very
conservative figure) and is currently worth $72,000.
The balance outstanding on your mortgage is $38,689 -
which gives you an equity of $33,311. That's a lot of
money to have sitting idle.

"If you refinanced or went in for a second mortgage, most
lenders today would probably lend you only 80 percent of
the value of your house, rather than the 90 percent you
got when mortgage money was available on easier terms.
That means you could borrow a total of $57,600 on the
house (80 percent of its present value of $72,000).
Since the outstanding balance on your mortgage is
$38,689, you can raise an additional $18,911 by refinancing your current mortgage, or by taking out a second one.

"As you can see from the chart below, you'll end up saving $53,353 in interest costs if you take out a second
mortgage. Granted, your combined monthly payments for
the second mortgage and the original mortgage will be
$131 a month higher than what you'd have to pay if you re-
financed your mortgage. (But you'll be able to increase
your tax deductions for interest.)

	Refinancing Your Mortgage vs.	Combination Original &	Second Mortgage
Amount of loan	$57,600	$38,689*	$18,911
Interest rate	9%	6.5%	12.5%
Length of loan	25 years	15 years	10 years
Monthly payment	$484	$338	$277
Interest cost over term of loan	$87,034	$19,386	$14,295
Fees	$2,000**	None	$15 to $150
Total monthly payments at beginning	$484		$615

18

Total interest cost	$87,034	$33,681

* Balance of original mortgage outstanding
**Fees could amount to $2,000 for new closing costs and
the possibility of a prepayment penalty.

"However, before you get a second mortgage, look into
other alternatives. Be sure to check out, for instance,
the terms on a loan for the special purpose you have in
mind. For example, education loans are often less costly
than a second mortgage loan might be, but might not be
made for as long a period."

The timing of borrowing money is important. Right now
we are approaching the peak in interest rates. Interest rates have about a four-year cycle. Thus, two years
from now, interest rates should be quite low again. Then
I look for the prime rate to be about 7%. So about a
year and a half from now (the fall of 1980) you can begin
to look around for a second mortgage for your home, or to
purchase rural property. By the time you consumate a
deal, the interest rates should be at just about their
bottom.

MCKEEVER'S RULE #3 FOR THE 1980'S:

*ANY INVESTMENT THAT IS NOT MAKING AT LEAST 5%
OVER THE INFLATION RATE SHOULD BE LIQUIDATED*

If you have borrowed (and improved your lending/borrow-
ing ratio) by purchasing rural property and so forth, you
are not concerned about what to do with the money. On
the other hand, if you have taken a second mortgage on
your home, and have cash in hand, there becomes a significant question as to what to do with it, so it will
at least keep up with inflation, and hopefully make some
profit on top of it. I have two suggestions:

1. *Be as liquid as possible.* I consider a liquid investment anything that you can sell within 5 minutes and have your money within 24 hours. Stocks,
   commodities, and gold and silver coins are all very
   liquid. Moving down the liquidity ladder, you pass
   stamps, diamonds and antiques. Real estate is low
   on the list, and equity in a private corporation is
   at the bottom, being most illiquid.

2. *Choose the risk level which allows you to sleep.*
With every investment there is a risk. If I buy an
antique desk, it could burn up, it could get broken
in moving or by children, the value of it could go
down, or it could be a copy and not a true antique.
You weigh such risks against the potential reward,
and when you have a risk/reward ratio that you are
comfortable with, that would be a good investment.
In something like the commodities market, the risk
is very high and the potential rewards are very high.
With the ups and downs in commodities, some people
are too nervous to be comfortable.

There will not be space in this issue to look at investments in real estate, stamps, diamonds, gold and silver
coins, numismatic coins, food and so forth. We hope to
be able to cover those in detail in the next issue of
MISL.

MCKEEVER'S RULE #4 FOR THE 1980'S:

> *BE SURE YOUR INCOME*
> *STAYS AHEAD OF THE INFLATION RATE*

Let's assume for the moment that the average salary in
the United States increased by the exact rate of inflation. Please note that this was the *average*. Thus,
those whose salary increases at less than the average,
lost purchasing power to inflation and those who's salary increased at a rate greater than the average, gained
purchasing power as related to inflation. What this says
is that at this minute if your salary is not increasing
at 15% a year, you are losing ground to inflation. If
you are a professional individual (many of our subscribers are doctors, lawyers, and so forth), you might look
at your fee schedule and determine whether your fees are
15% higher than they were last year. If they are not,
then you are losing ground to inflation. If you own
your own business, be sure to give yourself raises that
would compensate for inflation. If you are paid a salary by someone else, let your employer know that you are
aware of the inflation situation. For example, if you
are making $2,000 per month, with a $300 raise you would
simply break even with inflation. The amount of the

raise that is over $300 is really your increase. If you
are bashful about discussing these things with your employer, inflation will move income from you to someone
else who is not so bashful.

If you are not yet retired, be sure and examine your
retirement program and be sure that it is indexed to the
cost of living. Even if you have to put a little bit
more into the retirement policy to get the cost of living indexation, it would be well worth it.

SUMMARY AND CONCLUSION

I believe strongly that inflation will continue and
get worse. Therefore, I would encourage you to plan
your strategy around this fact. If you wish to listen
to the deflationists, to get confused by them and to
allow them to paralyze and neutralize you so that you
do nothing, then you will have your wealth transferred
away from you because of inflation.

To help avoid having wealth transferred away from you,
we would encourage you to have a lending/borrowing ratio
of as small a number as possible, keeping your borrowing
within the basic limit of 5 times your annual salary.
We then looked at any additional funds that are borrowed
to be invested in something that is going to keep ahead
of inflation. These investments should be as liquid as
possible, and they should have the risk/reward ratio
that will allow you to sleep comfortably at night.

By proper planning, and anticipating the inflation that
is coming, you can have wealth transferred *to* you rather
than *away* from you and your family.

More on

WORSE INFLATION

Reprinted from MISL #185, April 1979

You will beat inflation, or inflation will beat you. You had better consider this as a war, not just the moral equivalent of war, but a hot, full-fledged financial war. As in any war, if you do nothing, you will be defeated by the enemy. I realize that I am stating this quite strongly. My hope is that a strong statement will jar some of you into action.

In the last issue of MISL, we looked at some of the reasons why I felt inflation was going to continue and to get worse. We also looked at how inflation transfers wealth in various ways. One of these ways is a transfer from lenders to borrowers. In my thinking, it is not a matter of whether or not we will have more inflation, but simply how bad it will be across the next twenty years. The following table can help you in your thinking. This table shows how long it will take, at various inflation rates, for you to lose 50% of your purchasing power:

INFLATION RATE	YEARS TO LOSE 50% OF PURCHASING POWER
7%	10.2
8%	9.0
9%	8.0
10%	7.3
12%	6.1
15%	5.0
20%	3.8
25%	3.1
30%	2.6

At the 15% inflation rate, which we are running right now, this table says that *in just five years you will lose 50% of your purchasing power!* This means that if you have a life insurance policy and you were to die five years from now, at this inflation rate it would only buy 50% of what it would buy if you were to die today. If you have bonds, in five years their value will purchase only half of what it will purchase today. Thus, we see that our store of wealth (no matter how small or large your wealth is, we all have some) *must* keep ahead of inflation, or we will quickly lose the war to our financial archenemy number one, *INFLATION*.

I have frequently stated that I felt the average inflation rate for the next twenty years would be 12%. I am beginning to feel that this is low, and that it will probably average at least 15%. We will be using that as my estimate in the remainder of this article. This means that if you are not making 15% on an investment, you are not keeping up with inflation and you are losing your assets. Assuming that your realistic goal is to make at least 5% above the inflation rate, this means that today you must be making 20% on an investment to be making any profit at all. To help you evaluate your investments, in each issue of MISL we have a section called "Values-Indices-Prices (VIP)". This is usually the last item in the newsletter. For this issue we are reproducing it here, so that we can help you understand how to use it properly:

	Friday 4/6/79	Friday 3/30/79	Year Ago	% Chg	PAID
GOLD	$239.75	$240.10	$181.00	+32	17%
SILVER	7.50	7.43	5.27	+42	27%
GOLD SHARES (FTI)	107.30	108.10	98.10	+ 9	- 6%
DJIA	875.69	862.18	769.95	+14	- 1%
DJT (Transport)	234.08	225.17	206.86	+13	- 2%
DJSC (Spot Comm)	377.42	378.09	360.56	+ 5	-10%

COINS

AUSTRIAN 100 KORONA	246.00	245.75	188.00	+31	16%
KRUGERRAND	255.50	257.50	194.00	+32	17%
MEXICAN 50 PESO	307.50	309.25	236.50	+30	15%
SILVER COINS (bag)	5,580.00	5,580.00	3,940.00	+42	27%

As you can see from the VIP table, it gives the prices of these various items and indices for the last two Fridays, as well as for a year ago. It shows the percent change of the current price as contrasted to the price a year ago. Looking at this VIP table, we can see that if one year ago you put 100% of all of your wealth into gold, you would have made 32% gross over the last year (with 15% inflation, this would leave the Profit After Inflation Deducted - PAID - of 17%).

PAID is our new nomenclature for Profit After Inflation is Deducted, since this is the percentage you really get paid. If you had invested 100% in silver one year ago, you would get PAID 27%, since the percent change in price is 42%. If you had invested in South African gold shares, in the same mix as the Financial Times Index (FTI), published in London, the percent change in price is 9% and you would get PAID -6% (a 6% loss). If you had invested in the DJIA (stocks in the same ratio that composed the Dow Industrial Average) that change is 14% and you would get PAID -1%. If you had invested in the stocks that compose the Dow Jones Transportation average (DJT), the percent change in their value is 13% and you would get PAID -2%, and you would get PAID -10% on Spot Commodity Index (DJSC).

In the VIP section we have done a similar thing for
the most popular gold and silver coins. Here you can
see that these all fared quite nicely. However, this
was not always the case. Through most of 1975 and 1976
the percent change for gold, silver, gold shares and
the coins themselves was negative. On the other hand,
during those years, the percent change for the DJIA
and DJT were quite positive. This takes us to another
one of McKeever's rules:

MCKEEVER'S RULE #5 FOR THE 1980'S:

*YOU MUST SWITCH PERIODICALLY FROM ONE TYPE OF
INVESTMENT TO ANOTHER TO WIN OVER INFLATION*

At the beginning of 1975 we said to get out of gold.
About two years later, when gold was $115 an ounce,
we said to buy it, and then on November 1, 1978, we
again said to sell gold, and to move into the stock
market. These are the types of moves from market to
market that are required if one is going to be vic-
torious over inflation.

Now let's review some of these markets and also look at
some of the less popular areas for investments.

GOLD AND SILVER

We won't spend much time on the precious metals because
of past articles and the fact that most of our readers
know how I stand on gold and silver. If one were looking
for an investment that one could simply make and put
aside for five years - an investment that would have the
best chance of keeping up with inflation - I would say
that it would be silver.

If you bought gold when it was $200 at the end of 1974,
using an average inflation rate of 10%, the price of
gold today would have to be $292.82 *just to break even*.
If we needed to make 15% a year, which lets us get PAID
5%, gold today would have to be $349.80 to achieve this.
In this example, gold would not have kept up with infla-

tion. If you bought it at a much lower price, such as when we recommended it at $115, then it would have kept above inflation. You can further see how rule #5, about moving from one market to another, is very important.

If you look at silver across the same four-year period, if you had purchased it at the end of 1974, you would have paid $4.40. Today silver is $7.43. This gives us a net annual price change of 14%. Using our 10% average inflation rate across that period of time, we would get PAID 4% a year.

Many have written asking how they should hold gold and silver. I would say without hesitation, *only in coins*, in your possession, or in bullion at a Swiss bank. I would not buy any of the bars or commemorative medallions. I would only buy gold coins minted by some government, preferably in the one ounce size, such as the Krugerrand, the new Maple Leaf Canadian coin, or the one the U.S. government is planning to mint. I would only buy silver for delivery in the form of silver coins.

To have coins "in your possession" means that they are where you are. This could be a safe-deposit box in a bank, or on your own property. Remember the adage that a thief cannot steal what he cannot find. Many people hide them in their attics, in old paint cans, or in the bottom of potted plants where a thief would not find them. There are disadvantages, particularly to silver coins in that they are heavy and bulky. No one said that it was going to be easy. If you would like to lay aside something for a rainy day that is going to keep a store of value, I place silver coins at the top of the list.

If you do want to have some wealth stored outside of the country, you can have a Canadian or Mexican safe-deposit box where you can store gold or silver coins (not bullion). Another alternative is to have a Swiss bank buy for you gold or silver bullion (not coins). If they do this and *they* store it, they will guarantee that it is deliverable gold or silver. This is the only way that I would hold bullion bars.

We will deal with gold and silver futures contracts
when we discuss commodities.

THE STOCK MARKET

As far as a long-term investment hedge, you can forget
about the stock market. It basically peaked out in
1968 and has been moving sideways to downward ever
since. However, let me hasten to add that there is occasionally a two-year bull market in the stock market
and a great deal of money can be made by participating
in these. Many hard money investors, I believe, have
erroneously written off the stock market. Perhaps this
is because they lost money in it. But remember that
just because the horse bucks you off doesn't mean that
the horse is all bad.

Looking at the same four-year period that we looked at
for gold and silver, if one had bought the DJIA at the
end of 1974, he would have paid $634 for it. At today's
level of $878 this is an average annual price increase of
8.5% for which you would have gotten PAID a -1.5%.

BONDS, SAVINGS ACCOUNTS, LIFE INSURANCE POLICIES

We have said over and over again, *anything denominated
in a fixed amount of U.S. dollars is going to lose
against inflation*. Our advice is that you be out of all
of these, as far as investment is concerned. If you want
life insurance, buy term insurance; keep some cash on
hand for emergencies, but don't think of *investing* in any
of these entities.

COMMODITIES

There is by far more money to be made in the commodities
market than any of these other markets, but the risks
are proportionally high. The reason for this is because
of the high leverage in the commodity market. If you remember your high school physics, with the right leverage

a small force can lift a great weight. The force is mul-
tiplied.

Similarly, in the commodities market, say for a futures
contract in gold, you are required to put down (margin)
$1,500. This controls 100 ounces of gold. If gold
moves up $15, you will have doubled your money, and if
it moves down $15 you will have lost *all* of your money.
That magnitude of a gold movement can take place during
a single week. Thus, very quickly one can make enormous
profits or suffer enormous losses. The key to investing
in the commodities market is to realize that the majority
of your trades will probably lose, and therefore to cut
these loss positions quickly, and let the ones that are
profitable run.

Because of the high-risk/high-reward nature of commodities, I never suggest that anyone place more than 10% of
his liquid net assets in commodities. By placing 90%
of one's liquid net assets into other less leveraged investments, such as gold, silver, stocks, and real estate,
then to have an additional amount invested in commodities
could be an excellent balance to round out the investment
portfolio.

FOREIGN CURRENCIES

For some it might be difficult to think about "investing"
in foreign currencies, but today all currencies, including the U.S. dollar, are simply commodities. They are
no longer performing the true function of money. Some
people have thought of the Swiss franc as an inflation
hedge. This is not true when you apply hard facts to
it. It is true that it has fared better than the U.S.
dollar, but at the beginning of 1975 the Swiss franc
was worth $.43. Today it is worth $.58. Using the
same calculation as we have in our other areas of investments, this gives us an annual rate of price appreciation of 7.8%. Calculating in our average inflation
rate of 10% during this period, you actually got PAID
-1.2% for investing in Swiss francs. A great deal of

money was made in Swiss francs, primarily in the Swiss franc futures market. There was a time to buy and then came a time to sell (our flash sell signal on November 1, 1978). Remember, we must move in and out of these markets at appropriate times in order to win each battle against inflation, so as to win this very real war.

REAL ESTATE

Here we are looking purely at *investing* in real estate. We are not looking at owning your own home, which we covered in the last issue of MISL, or at a doctor owning the building in which his practice is located. That is the type of real estate which one buys and intends to hold. What we are talking about here is real estate which one buys and intends to sell within four or five years.

Before we begin, let me restate the big negative in real estate. *It is not liquid*. Whereas almost all the other investments we have talked about in this issue, you can sell within five minutes, real estate could take five months or more to sell. This creates a bit of financial immobility that one has to consider, if one is going to invest in real estate.

Assuming that we want to get PAID at least 5%, this means that on any real estate we buy, we are going to have to double our money in four or five years. I did not say double the value of the real estate. I said double our money. For example, if one were able to buy a $50,000 house at 10% down, $5,000, then he would have to be able to sell the house within four or five years for $55,000 in order to give himself a $5,000 profit, which would double his original investment. This is assuming that the rental received on the house would cover all closing costs, payments, interest and so forth. (A $5,000 profit after five years would be a 20% a year return on one's money minus 15% inflation, PAID 5%.)

By properly shopping around, one can find properties that

29

have an eager seller and are undervalued. For example,
if someone has died and his heirs are eager to dispose
of a piece of real estate in order to settle the estate,
you can frequently negotiate a small downpayment, good
terms on paying it out (including an assignable mortgage)
and get it for a price somewhat under its appraised
value. This type of real estate investment is covered
well in John Kamin's book, *How to Make Money Fast Specu-
lating in Distressed Property* (published by Pyramid
Books). He deals with buying property at auctions, from
banks that have foreclosed, and so forth. One can often
get good bargains and make substantial profits in this
area.

Another avenue of real estate investment that I believe
will continue to do well is operating farms. These can
be either small or large operations, but with all of
the outbuildings and necessary supplies. In southern
Oregon, the value of this type of property is going up
at about 25% a year. That is on the total value. From
our earlier example, if one were able to pay $5,000 down
on a $50,000 farm, and it went up in value 25% per year,
this would mean that in four years the farm would be
worth $100,000! If one broke even on all expenses, the
$5,000 would have brought in an incredible $45,000 profit! This would have kept well ahead of inflation.

DIAMONDS, STAMPS, ANTIQUES, ART

Some of these areas can keep ahead of inflation and you
can have a lot of fun at them, if you know what you are
doing. We will try to cover these in a future issue of
MISL, but space does not allow us to go into them at
this point.

SUMMARY AND CONCLUSION

We have seen that to win in the war that INFLATION is
waging against you, you need to be PAID (Profit After
Inflation Deducted) at least 5%. This means 5% over the
inflation rate. Thus, today any investment not making

20% per year should be liquidated and the funds moved into other investment areas. However, one cannot be static. What is making better than 20% this year, two years from now may be losing 20% a year. One needs to move periodically out of one investment area into another.

For a long-term, "buy-it-and-forget-it" investment to keep ahead of inflation, the only thing seems to be silver. This should be held either in bullion form in a Swiss bank, or in coin form in your own possession.

In any war a general must know his present status and continually monitor the evolving situation in order to win. Thus, we would encourage you to sit down and calculate what each of your investments PAID during 1978. Then rearrange your investments so that you are making, on the average, more than 20% per year. Monitor these, say once a quarter, to make adjustments as they are required. Of course here in MISL we will give you signals when we see major changes in markets coming. We are on your side and want to do everything we can to help.

3

THE TURTLE vs. THE RABBIT

Reprinted from MISL #174, September 1978

Everyone today seems to be in a hurry. I have the privilege of consulting with many doctors, and almost universally one of their main concerns is that they are eager to retire as soon as possible. They want to make a bundle *fast* in order to achieve this. Unfortunately, they frequently make investments that prove to be unsound, in hopes of doubling their money, or they invest in tax shelter schemes that in the long run turn out to be almost worthless. They frequently would have been better off either paying their taxes or giving that money to charity. A tax shelter investment must first be a good, sound investment; if it also has tax benefits, so much the better. Perhaps one of the reasons for some of these kinds of investment decisions is that some of these doctors are in such a hurry that they do not have long-term goals and a long-term strategy.

I don't mean to be picking on the doctors; they are simply typical of individuals in many occupations. But while I'm on the subject of the doctors, it is interesting to note that a doctor will spend a number of years in college and medical school. After this he has the years of his internship and residency. Then he takes a few years to build a practice and possibly acquire some equipment. In total, he perhaps invests 15 years or so in getting to a point in his life at which all of a sudden he finds himself with some surplus funds. He then goes out to invest them. Perhaps he reads a book or two, and talks to a couple of people before he invests. The total amount of time devoted to his "investment training and education" might be as much as 15 hours. He is competing against investors who have spent 20 to 30 years learning the investment business, and he wonders why he frequently loses. Newsletters such as this and investment conferences are designed to attempt to fill in the gaps in one's investment training.

On the other end of the spectrum, there are people who are already retired and are living primarily on a fixed income. They may have sold their larger home, purchased either a condominium or a smaller home and put the difference into a savings account or bonds. Unfortunately, with inflation running at about 10% a year and these investments paying 5% to 8% a year, people such as this are losing a portion of their capital every month. The U.S. government, by creating inflation, has told these people that they can no longer save, at least in U.S. dollars, but instead they must invest. They, too, have had little investment training and this is a frightening world to them. They need the same help as professionals, like doctors, but for very different reasons. One of the purposes of MISL is to help give some guidance and evaluate various investment opportunities for a more productive long-range strategy.

THE FUTURE OF THE U.S. DOLLAR IS A KEY

As we begin to look at an intelligent, longer-range strategy of gradually adding to our wealth and "getting rich slowly", we must deal with the inflation question. If inflation is going to continue and get worse over the next 5 to 20 years, this significantly affects our long-range planning.

For the sake of the many new readers, who have joined us because of the radio and television appearances that I have made recently, we need to quickly review the causes of future inflation. My favorite way to explain it is as follows: If you had a group of friends in your living room and I came in and passed out some monoply money to all of these people and held an auction of all the various items in the living room (the pictures, tables, chairs and so forth), we would come up with one level of prices. What would happen if I passed out exactly twice as much monoply money to those same people and held the same auction? The prices of the various items would roughly be doubled.

In an oversimplified manner, when you read that the U.S. government is deficit spending by $50 billion, the net result is that they are passing out "extra monoply money" to the tune of $50 billion, and this forces prices up. Prices will continue to rise as long as the government deficit spends, and thus is forced to increase its money supply.

If the U.S. government were to start balancing its budget and paying off the national debt, and thus stop its deficit spending, inflation would either level off or decline back down to about 2% or 3% a year. However, if the government continues to deficit spend and not even attempt to liquidate the national debt, you can be assured that inflation will be with us, and in a strong way, for many years to come. Your evaluation as to which way the government will perform in this matter is critical in your planning.

I have been warning about the coming inflation for a year now. At the end of 1977, in my predictions for 1978, I said (MISL #159):

> "I think that inflation is going to resume next year (1978) with fury. I believe that many people, and the U.S. government, are going to be shocked when it really hits as bad as I think it will. The reasons

34

for this are multitudinous. *First you have the tremendous U.S. dollar devaluation that has occurred
during 1977. This will raise the price of all imported goods by about 20%."*

Just as an aside while we are on the subject, in that
same December, 1977 issue, I pointed out what to do about
this:

*"To take advantage of the U.S. dollar demise, in the
commodity futures market, you could buy contracts in
Swiss francs, Deutsche marks and Japanese yen. I am
particularly impressed with the Japanese yen. . . .*

*"In order to take advantage of or profit out of the
coming rise in interest rates, in the commodity futures you would want to sell short T-bills and Gin-
nie Maes."*

I am sure that all of you who followed this advice are
today very happy with the results and have made far
more than enough money to justify your receiving MISL.
In fact, you may remember that back in August of 1977 I
recommended the purchasing of these key foreign currencies.

Back to inflation . . . For many many reasons I believe
that there is significant inflation ahead of us and that
it will be far worse than what we have experienced up to
this point. There will be ups and downs in the inflation
rate, but with each cycle the inflation rate peak is going to get higher and higher. By the year 2000, it would
not surprise me to see the average inflation rate at
about 30%! So my recommendation is that you factor bigger (and better?) inflation into the development of your
long-term strategy.

LONG-RANGE GOAL . . . RETIRE IN STYLE

Some people have short-range investment goals, such as
making a quick $20,000 for a partial payment on the boat

or a trip to Europe, or some other immediate expenditure. However, for almost everyone, our longer-range goal should probably read something like this:

> *My long-range goal is to invest now so that my investments will keep ahead of inflation, plus a return, in order that I can have a high level income when I retire.*

If you have already retired, you would want to modify that slightly to read:

> *My long-range goal is to have my investments (including savings) keep ahead of inflation, plus a return, so that I can at least maintain, and hopefully improve, my standard of living.*

With these goals in mind, it becomes obvious that one must be making at least 13% on any investment - that is, the 10% inflation rate plus at least a 3% return on an investment. Thus, at least for the present rates of inflation, if you are making between 13% and 20% on your *average* investment, you are achieving this long-term objective. You can have some money in lower paying investments such as CD's, savings accounts and bonds, if you have a corresponding investment that it providing a higher rate of return, so that the *average* rate of return is a minimum of 13%. Now let us look at some of the places where you can invest, or save, and achieve this type of return.

SAVING IN A MEDIUM THAT RETAINS ITS VALUE

In the last issue, MISL #173, we discussed how essential saving is. However, the saving must not be done in the form of U.S. dollars. The question then comes: What else is there that is quite liquid that one can save? In the last issue we suggested silver coins, gold coins and Swiss francs (in order of my preference). If you are a new subscriber and did not receive that issue, we will be happy to send you a complimentary copy.

36

After that issue, some of our subscribers wrote in asking
how they could save in Swiss francs if they did not want
to open a Swiss bank account. There are two ways that
this can be done. One is to go to almost any international bank and buy traveler's checks denominated in
Swiss francs. The other way is to actually purchase the
currency. This can be done in most international air-
ports, or you can write to:

    Nicholas Deak, President
    Deak & Company
    29 Broadway
    New York, NY 10006

This company is the number one dealer in the U.S. in
foreign currencies. They have offices in most major
cities and Nicholas Deak will be happy to send you the
address of the office nearest you. Through Deak & Company, actual Swiss franc currency can be obtained. The
Swiss franc currency or the Swiss franc denominated
traveler's checks can be kept in a safe-deposit box, or
in whatever safe place one desires.

In any one of these three types of saving media (silver
coins, gold coins and Swiss francs), the price, as measured in U.S. dollars, can fluctuate. What if the price
went down for a year or two? Should one stop saving in
these precious metals or Swiss francs? The answer is
not only should one continue to save in these if their
price is declining, but possibly even double the amount
of savings while the price is low. This principle is
called cost averaging. I would like to take an example
of it.

COST AVERAGING

In cost averaging, an investor buys a number of coins
or shares of a stock at various prices. He is hoping,
then, to have a low average cost of purchase so that
he will maximize his profit when he sells. For example,
let's say that the value of a Krugerrand (a one ounce

gold coin) was $200 and that it declined $5 every month, until a year later it was worth $145, and then it began to appreciate $5 each month so that 12 months later it was again at $200. Buying one Krugerrand a month in this instance would have a cost as follows:

		Year 1	Year 2
Month	1	$200	$145
	2	195	150
	3	190	155
	4	185	160
	5	180	165
	6	175	170
	7	170	175
	8	165	180
	9	160	185
	10	155	190
	11	150	195
	12	145	200

By purchasing one Krugerrand each month during this entire two-year period, the average purchase price would be $172.50. By the time the two-year cycle was over, and the Krugerrand was once again worth $200, the average coin would have appreciated in value 16%.

There are a number of other schemes that can be used in cost averaging. For example, one could say that if the price of Krugerrands gets to $170 or less, 2 coins each month will be purchased. If one followed that plan in this case, the average purchase price would be $168. Another plan would be to invest $200 a month and allow any surplus to accumulate until an extra coin could be bought. In this case, the average purchase price would be $171. All three of these average purchase prices are so close that it seems to me that the simplest and cleanest would be to purchase one Krugerrand each month.

In the last issue, I said that I preferred silver coins over gold coins for a saving medium. I believe the action of the last couple of weeks has already validated that, because we have seen gold drop substantially and silver hold up and even rise a little bit. I believe that silver will outperform gold even more so across the next few years, and we are thinking in terms of longer-range planning here. Thus, at the top of my preference list, I would still recommend saving regularly in silver coins. We said last time that a $100,000 house can be bought today with 20,000 silver dollars. This certainly is in keeping with our stated long-term goals.

LONG-RANGE INVESTING

Most of the long-range investments are illiquid, which is a negative for them. (I consider a liquid investment anything that you can sell within 15 minutes and get your money within 24 hours.) If one's long-term investments are going to be wise investments, with the present rate of inflation they must be appreciating at 13% a year, or hopefully more. Some which might fit into this category at the present time are:

Real Estate (excluding residence): In most areas of the country, real estate in general is keeping ahead of the inflation rate. However, with rising interest rates and a sharply rising real estate market, many people are expressing concern that this bubble could burst, at least temporarily. The best returns in real estate appear to be in finding property that is somewhat run down in an otherwise good neighborhood, fixing it up and then either renting it or selling it.

Raw land: In many areas raw land has been appreciating more than the inflation rate. For example, in Oregon it has been going up at approximately 25% a year for the last several years. I've been recommending for several years purchasing farm land or working farms. I believe these will continue to appreciate ahead of inflation. However, at this point in time I would not recommend the purchasing of raw land on the speculation that it might become valuable for a subdivision or a shopping center.

Art and antiques: These investments are ones that you can enjoy while they appreciate. However, they could prove to be some of the most illiquid of all investments, since in a time of monetary crunch, these objects may well indeed be *worth* a great deal but there simply may not be any buyers.

Private company shares: These would be shares in a company that is not publicly traded. It may be a business that one has started, a family business or the incorporation of a doctor's(s') practice. These shares in a private company are also very illiquid and almost impossible to sell. However, if it involves your livelihood, it may be one of the best investments that you have.

Other long-term investments: There are many other long-term investments, such as rare stamps, rare (numismatic) coins and so forth which fit into the same category as art and antiques. You could also place diamonds in this category. I will not deal with the subject of diamonds in depth at this point (perhaps in a future issue). Suffice it to say that one must both *know* this market and realize that it is a controlled market: DeBeers own about 30% of the diamonds and they are the ones who set the price.

INVESTING IN STOCKS AND COMMODITIES

The most popular investments are stocks and commodities. In every issue we have a stock market section, so we will not be discussing this in depth at this point. However, I would like to say a word about commodities. Most people are afraid of commodities, having heard the gruesome stories of people losing large amounts in commodities. It is interesting to note that commodities alone are really beating inflation. The following is part of an ad by a commodity investment firm (Comvest, 5 Broadway, Saugus, MA 01906). In it they show, for the period 1969-1978, what various investments have returned above or below the average annual inflation rate of 7.4%:

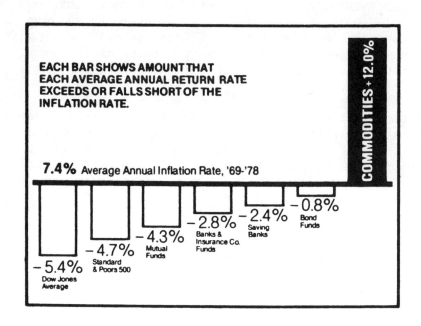

This chart shows why our Model Portfolio and the money I manage for clients is invested primarily in the comodities market. Had gold, silver and Swiss francs (all of which are commodities) been shown individually on these graphs, they would have done the best of all.

Most people do not understand commodities. One well-known movie star, who has been a subscriber to MISL since it began, wrote and asked that I explain more about commodities. We will have an upcoming issue on commodities for those people who would like to understnad this market better. In the interim, there is a back issue, MISL #120, entitled "Understanding Commodities" that could be of real help to you. (This will be sent to anyone contributing $3 or more.)

CALCULATE YOUR NET WORTH - BY MCKEEVER'S METHOD

Most calculations of net worth are confusing to the average person and are not useful as a planning tool. One reason for this is that the assets and liabilities are listed on top of each other and the net worth of any one item is difficult to ascertain. Another reason is that most people don't know really what their financial situation is, even if they have an accountant, because of the accounting practices required by the U.S. government. Assets must be shown at the purchase price and not the market value. Thus, if a stock was purchased high and is worthless today, it still shows a great deal of value on the balance sheet. Similarly, something purchased for a song that has appreciated significantly, adds no value to your balance sheet. If you purchased a 20-story building for $1 from your Uncle, you could never show that building as valued more than $1 as an asset on your balance sheet. (But your property tax would be based on market value!)

To help you get a realistic picture of your financial situation, we are including, on page 4, the Net Worth Form (McKeever's Method) that I use in my consultations. Once the true situation is determined, then and only then can planning for the redistribution of one's investments be made intelligently. I would encourage you to take some time and to fill out this form, for your own sake.

Let me say a word or two about this form. Under the category of "Savings", we have listed only those things that I consider true savings, at this point in time. These are items that are 100% paid for and are in your possession or immediately accessible to you. In a previous issue (MISL #169), I encouraged you to separate your gold and silver coins into two categories - investments and insurance. The insurance portion should be shown here under savings.

Under the "Liquid Investments" are all of the shorter-term investments that you fully intend to sell for prof-

MARKET VALUE NET WORTH FORM --- MCKEEVER'S METHOD

NET WORTH OF (Name)_____ As of (Date)_____

NOTE: Amounts to be expressed in thousands of dollars. $10,518 should be written as $10.5.	MARKET VALUE $ (A)	DEBT AMOUNT $ (B)	NET VALUE $ (C)	PERCENT NET (D)	GOAL PERCENT (E)	GOAL $ (F)
SAVINGS						
(1) Silver Coins in Possession	$.	$.	$.	. %	. %	$.
(2) Gold Coins in Possession	.	.	.	.	.	.
(3) Swiss Francs	.	.	.	.	.	.
(4) TOTAL SAVINGS	.	.	.	.	.	.
INVESTMENTS - LIQUID						
(5) Gold Bullion and Coins on margin	.	.	.	.	.	.
(6) Silver Bullion and Coins on margin	.	.	.	.	.	.
(7) Foreign Currency Accounts	.	.	.	.	.	.
(8) Gold Mining Shares	.	.	.	.	.	.
(9) Equity Shares	.	.	.	.	.	.
(10) Gold Futures	.	.	.	.	.	.
(11) Silver Futures	.	.	.	.	.	.
(12) Currency Futures	.	.	.	.	.	.
(13) Commodity Futures - Other	.	.	.	.	.	.
(14) Other_____	.	.	.	.	.	.
(15) Other_____	.	.	.	.	.	.
(16) TOTAL INVESTMENTS-LIQUID	.	.	.	.	.	.
INVESTMENTS - ILLIQUID (LONG TERM)						
(17) Real Estate (Exclude Residence)	.	.	.	.	.	.
(18) Raw Land	.	.	.	.	.	.
(19) Art and Antiques	.	.	.	.	.	.
(20) Private Company Shares	.	.	.	.	.	.
(21) Other_____	.	.	.	.	.	.
(22) TOTAL INVESTMENTS - ILLIQUID	.	.	.	.	.	.
INVESTMENTS - STATIC (INCLUDE INCOME PRODUCING)						
(23) Cash in Banks	.	.	.	.	.	.
(24) Bonds, T-Bills, CD's	.	.	.	.	.	.
(25) Residence	.	.	.	.	.	.
(26) Rental Property	.	.	.	.	.	.
(27) Retreat and Food Storage	.	.	.	.	.	.
(28) Loans - Personal	.	.	.	.	.	.
(29) Other_____	.	.	.	.	.	.
(30) TOTAL INVESTMENTS - STATIC	.	.	.	.	.	.
GRAND TOTAL AND NET WORTH	$.	$.	$. (Net Worth)	100.0%	100.0%	$.

CALCULATION OF NET WORTH IN TERMS OF GOLD AND SILVER

Gold $_____/ounce. Net Worth in ounces of Gold _____ounces.

Silver $_____/ounce. Net Worth in ounces of Silver _____ounces.

it. Under the "Illiquid Investments", we have included the long-term investments that we have just discussed.

There is a fourth category, "Static Investments." These are investments that possibly are not even keeping up with inflation. Here we have included all of the things that are in fixed dollar amounts, such as cash and bonds. We have also included rental property, since frequently one is buying a cash flow (income) and is not so much looking at it as an investment. The value of one's residence may or may not be keeping up with inflation and may or may not be a wise investment, so we have placed it in this category. Frequently a residence is bought and retained, not because it is a good invest-ment, but simply because one enjoys it and *wants* to live there.

As we pointed out earlier, unlike normal U.S. accounting practice, where only the purchase price of an item can be shown as an asset, on this form you use the present mar-ket value. In order to determine this, you may actually have to have some real estate and antiques appraised.

Step 1: The present market value for all of your assets should be entered in column (A).

Step 2: In column (B) you should enter any loans against those items.

Step 3: Subtract column (B) from column (A). This gives the net value of *each item*. Enter this in column (C).

Step 4: Total column (C). This will be your net worth.

Step 5: In column (D) calculate what percentage each item is of the total net worth. This can be determined by dividing each item in column (C) by the total net worth figure.

Step 6: After looking at these percentages, you might

be in a state of shock. For example, at today's market price most people have far more tied up in their residence than they realize. You may decide that you would like to readjust some of these investments and shift them from one category to another. In column (E) you can write in your new desired (or goal) percentages.

Step 7: Translate these to an actual dollar figure in column (F), by multiplying the percent in column (E) by your net worth.

By completing this form, you are beginning to do some longer-range planning to insure that your investments are in a proper balance.

At the bottom of this form there is a place where you can enter the price of gold and the price of silver, as of the time that you did your net worth calculation. By dividing each of these figures into your net worth, you get your net worth in terms of ounces of silver and gold. If you do one of these net worth calculations every six months, and track to see if your net worth is rising or falling in terms of ounces of gold and silver, it should give you a solid base on which to measure the increase or decrease in your net worth, which could be falsely optimistic because of inflation.

As you will notice, we have given permission on the bottom of this form for any MISL subscriber to reproduce this page for his own personal use only. This is in case you would like to make several copies so that you can do this calculation every six months. The reason this permission is given is because it is now a criminal act to xerox pages of copyrighted newsletters.

SHOULD I BORROW TO INVEST?

I am frequently asked whether a person should refinance his house and invest the proceeds, and similar questions. This is probably one of the most difficult questions that

I am asked, because it so depends on the individual's
total financial picture and short-term and long-term ob-
jectives. Another factor to figure into this decision is
the interest rate cycle.

At the end of last year I projected in MISL #159 that we
would see significantly higher interest rates than people
are anticipating. That has proven to be true. I believe
that we will see these interest rates climb a little bit
higher before peaking out next year. Then we should see
about a two-year decline in interest rates and should experience interest rates far lower than people anticipate.
Thus, if one were going to do any borrowing to invest,
the time to do it would be about two years from now.
(Remember, we are dealing in long term here.)

There are also items that you would want to have 100%
paid for and never borrow against them. One of these
things might be your long-term gold and silver coins.
Another might be a duplex that you had purchased for a
retirement insurance. I mentioned in a previous issue
a German lady who lived through a runaway inflation, a
depression and a war in Germany by having a paid-for duplex. She lived in one half of it and the rent from the
other half bought her food. These types of "insurance"
investments should never have debt against them.

On the other hand, if one performs this net worth calculation and realizes that 80% of the net worth is tied up
in equity in a house, then serious reevaluation might be
in order. If one decides to refinance the house or to
take a second lien on it, the timing in connection with
the interest rate cycle would be critical. When refinancing, be sure that the only asset pledged to that loan
is the property, or the item itself, and none of your
other assets. Insist on this. It could be your salva-
tion if the bottom drops out.

BE A TURTLE AND WIN

So many people today have a desire to get rich quick, but

like the rabbit in the story, they wind up losing. What
I am encouraging people to do is to save (approximately
10% of your income) in terms of something of value and to
invest for the long haul, so that you can keep ahead of
inflation, and make money on top of it.

Our long-term goals are to be able to retire in style. A
well-thought-out savings and investment program should
allow us to do this. It is the better part of wisdom not
to rely on the government to take care of you during retirement, but to provide for yourself.

One of the keys to our long-range planning is your view
of the future, concerning inflation. I believe that in
coming years, inflation will not only remain with us, but
it will get worse. Thus, wise investments and saving become even more important. We looked at mediums in which
one could place one's savings so that inflation would not
eat them up, such as silver coins, gold coins, and Swiss
francs.

We also encouraged you to calculate your *Market Value Net
Worth* (or have your accountant do it), and then, after
determining your true net worth, to reevaluate the distribution of your assets. When considering the redistribution of those investments, some obviously need to be
placed in long-term investments and savings, and others
need to be placed wisely in more liquid short-term investments to take advantage of the major movements of the
markets.

By good planning today and wise investments and saving,
the economic cloud that hangs over America and the world
can have a silver lining for you.

4

Be Prepared for

A DEPRESSION

Reprinted from MISL #177, November 1978

I frequently get asked the question, "Do you think we are going to have another depression?" The answer that I usually give to this is: "Yes, we will have another depression, and it will be worse than the one that began in 1929, because it will be of a totally different type." The depression we had in 1929 was a traditional depression, or a *deflationary depression*. The one that is ahead of us will be a new kind - an *inflationary depression*. These two types of depressions were outlined excellently by Gary North in his newsletter, *Remnant Review*, (November 18, 1977, 713 W. Cornwallis Rd., Suite 100, Durham, NC 27707). Gary said:

"The characteristics of the traditional depression include these features:

1. falling prices
2. reduced output of goods and services
3. reduction of the money supply, because of
4. runs on banks that topple the fractional reserve pyramid of credit money

48

5. unemployed resources, including people
6. falling investment which results in
7. falling interest rates.

"The depression is a massive correction of the free market
to prior interventions by the government into the money
supply, namely, a prior monetary inflation. When Professor Ludwig von Mises was once asked by a student what
the government should have done about the depression, he
replied: 'Nothing . . . earlier.' If the government in-
tervenes, especially by creating price controls in the
form of price and wage *floors*, then the duration of the
effects of the depression will be extended, since the response of men to unemployment - the offering of their resources and serivces at lower prices - is made illegal
by the goverment. Men are then faced with continuing unemployment, or the sale of their below-legal price resources in the black markets. In fact, they have to offer these resources at far lower rates, to compensate the
buyers for the risks the latter bear in hiring this be-
low-floor labor or product. This is exactly the position
of the Mexican immigrant laborer today. What I have de-
scirbed is a traditional *deflationary depression*. It is
this form of depression that all Keynesian economists
think their policies can overcome. It is the depression
of falling prices and falling aggregate demand. Their
answer: more fiat money to finance purchases by government and those in cahoots with the government.

"Today we face a new kind of depression, the *inflationary
depression*, meaning the kind of depression which results
directly from the policies of the Keynesians. The Keynesians are absolutely baffled by this phenomenon. They
have no theoretical tools to use on this kind of depression. The features of the modern, Keynesian depression are these:

1. rising prices
2. slowing and then reduced output of goods and services
3. increase of the money supply, the result of

4. the creation of fiat money by the Federal Reserve System to finance
5. the increasing Federal budget deficit
6. unemployed resources, including people; reduced or falling investment which results in
7. falling short-term interest rates, that are followed by
8. rising long-term interest rates that are the result of
9. the increasing inflation premium tacked onto long-term loans by lenders who are trying to evade the effects of a depreciating currency unit.

"The traditional Keynesian solutions to 'depression' only add gosoline to the fire: more government spending, larger Federal deficits, and more fiat money. The intensity of the trade cycle increases. It takes more and more inflation to bring the unemployment rate back down, but only to increasingly high levels. Both unemployment rates and price inflation rates become 'ratcheted', never falling back to earlier levels."

RISING PRICES DURING THE DEPRESSION

Just to be sure that none of our readers have missed what we are saying, there is a depression of major magnitude ahead of us. However, prices will not drop like they did in 1929; instead, prices will skyrocket. Before we get into an analysis of why I am projecting this, (and I'm not alone; joined with me are a whole host of respected economic thinkers, such as Dr. Gary North, and Jerome Smith), we need first to turn our attention to the timing of this depression. The closer it is, the more we need to be concerned - right?

As we discussed in the last issue of MISL (which is an extremely important issue and I trust that everyone has read it carefully), the business environment runs in cycles of about 4 years: there is a 2-year business

growth followed by about 2 years of business recession.
In recent cycles, during the time of business growth inflation has become a problem, and consequently the government begins to fight inflation. As always they tend
to go overboard and fight it too much, and this amplifies the recession which is to follow. Then they begin
to fight the recession by pumping in additional funds,
which in turn amplifies the inflationary problem of the
next business recovery leg. As we said in the last
issue, *the key to knowing when the government has switch-
ed from fighting inflation to fighting a recession is in
the federal discount rate.* At present they are fighting
inflation, but my projection is that before 1980 is over,
they will reverse this and begin to fight a recession.

The government's cure for a recession is to pump in additional funds, give tax rebates to the citizens and so
forth, in order to "stimulate" private business. However, I think that a business recession will occur sometime between now and the year 2000 that it will be so
severe that the government will try to spend its way
out of it, but will be unable to stimulate the economy
in spite of all that it does. That recession will turn
into a major depression. However, there is no indication
that prices will not continue to increase through this
depression.

I do not look for the recession that we have predicted
for 1979 to turn into a depression. Beyond that, it is
difficult to project exactly *which* recession might continue the sled ride downward into a depression. We know
that we are living on borrowed time, so with each recession, the probability is getting greater and greater that
it will be the one to turn into a depression. For a number of reasons (discussed in MISL #161, "The Danger
Years, 1981 and 1982"), I am very leery of the recession
that will probably occur in 1982-1983. I would certainly
want to have my house in "depression-proof status" prior
to 1981.

LONG-RANGE PLANNING FOR AN INFLATIONARY DEPRESSION

It is difficult for most people to get excited about planning for or preparing for an event that *might* take place 4 years from now. Hence, most people do nothing. However, it is the ones who do take the time and effort to do the planning and preparation who will fare well during the inflationary depression that I see coming. There are a number of areas that one would need to consider in planning for this depression:

1. *Businesses and vocations* that would do well in a depression
2. *Investments* that would do well in an inflationary depression
3. *Residence* - location and financial status of it

DEPRESSION-FAVORED BUSINESSES

If one pauses for a minute to analyze a depression, one will conclude that people would have less purchasing power. As a result, people would tend *not* to buy new items, but rather to have old items repaired. Many would raise their own food and make their own home repairs. If one thinks through what happens when people have less purchasing power, one can ascertain for oneself which businesses would do well and which businesses would do poorly during a depression.

In the *Inflation Survival Letter*, September 6, 1978 (5809 Annapolis Rd., P.O. Box 2599, Landover Hills, MD 20784), Donald J. Hoppe wrote an excellent article entitled, "Inflation-Depression Proof Businesses". In it he said:

"There are businesses that do well *because* of a depression. Businesses that often *benefit* from a depression are: air conditioning service and repairs, used cars, auto repairs and auto parts, home cleaning services and supplies, gardening equipment and supplies, machine

tools, building repair and do-it-yourself equipment
and supplies of all types. Unlike an inflation era,
when people are quite willing to spend, a depression
causes the opposite - a money preference or determina-
tion to save.

"Money, during a depression, becomes scarce and highly
desirable, because it is generally *increasing* in value,
or at least holding its own. With most people facing an
uncertain economic future, the desire to limit expenses
and build up cash reserves becomes acute. Consequently,
the entrepreneur who can offer the public ways to cut
costs and save money will prosper. During a depression
there is a strong tendency to *repair* and rehabilitate
existing equipment rather than to buy new. There is also very little new building construction, either resi-
dential or commercial, but contractors and tradesmen
willing to concentrate on remodeling and redecorating
can survive.

"Barber and beauty shops also keep busy during a depression, not only because people want to look well to help
their morale and improve chances of finding employment,
but also because they have more time to spend in such
activities! To succeed, however, such services must
be offered at modest prices. Cheap entertainment is also much in demand, and that helps bowling alleys, inexpensive restaurants and resorts, breweries, sporting
goods manufacturers and retailers, camping equipment
suppliers and arts and crafts shops. Because there is
great concern about money and many financial problems,
small loan companies, pawn shops, bill collectors and
collection agencies, credit bureaus, financial advisory
services and auctioneers thrive during a depression.
Printing, advertising, public relations and sales promotion businesses are also among the beneficiaries of a
business turndown; the worse things get, the more
businessmen are inclined to advertise. They tend to concentrate on the less expensive print mediums rather than
on radio and TV, however.

"Leasing and rental services of all sorts enjoy increased

patronage during a depression. Because of the scarcity of cash and the general uncertainty regarding the future, consumers and businessmen alike are more inclined to lease or rent rather than to buy automobiles and trucks, machinery and tools, office equipment, typewriters, etc. Mail order businesses are almost depression-proof if the management concentrates on low-priced 'bargain' merchandise. Publishing benefits from hard times because people have more time to read and production costs can often be reduced.

"Most consumer-oriented businesses can survive a depression, provided that overhead can be trimmed and the company is not trapped in a bad long-term property lease, or has an unsupportable burden of debt service. However, there are certain areas that are hit hard by a recession or depression and should be avoided, as far as possible, during such times. These include private aircraft, new automobiles, boats and marinas, emloyment agencies, luxury entertainment, flowers and shrubbery, furs, jewelry, luggage, musical instruments, new office equipment and office machines, rugs and carpets, stamps and coins, live theater, taxis, travel agencies, hotels and motels and recreational vehicles."

Don's analysis is of a conventional depression, where people save and try to acquire cash. However, the same types of businesses do well in either type of depression. In an inflationary depression, one would not have the concern that Don expresses about long-term leases, and debt; in fact one would want them. As can be seen in Don's analysis, the luxury businesses and those requiring large capital expenditures will not fare well during a depression, whereas businesses oriented toward services will do much better. Thus, if one were going to do long-range planning and preparation for a depression, one would now begin to phase out of businesses designed for prosperous times and begin to move towards operating in businesses that are more service oriented.

Another factor to consider is this: with an unemployment

rate likely to go to 25%, there will be many highly-paid,
highly-qualified people in the unemployed ranks. Many
of them will want to start their own businesses for the
first time. Hopefully these people will have been wise
enough to have saved substantial amounts of their income
(hopefully in gold and silver coins) so that they will
have the capital necessary to start their own business.
A service to help people start their own businesses might
do extremely well during this depression.

DEPRESSION-FAVORED VOCATIONS

It should be obvious that vocations involving the service industries would be good ones to be in, whereas
vocations more involved with the luxury businesses would
not be so desirable. The medical profession should do
well during a depression; however, an increasing number
of people will turn to self-diagnosis and self-prescribed
remedies. Also there would be a growing trend toward
health foods and various other things to keep a person
healthy. A vocation such as design engineers may not be
as desirable since companies will not be interested so
much in designing and marketing new products, as they
will be in the continued marketing of existing products.
Salesmen will be in demand, if they produce.

The above has been just a sampling of vocations. Each
individual needs to examine his own vocation to see how
it would be affected if the populace and the government
had approximately 25% less purchasing power than they do
today. If you are in a vocation that is essential, it
is likely to be depression proof. If you are in a vocation that would not be so critical, given a reduction in
purchasing power, your employment could be somewhat in
jeopardy during a depression.

Remember, this will not be a traditional depression, but
rather an inflationary depression. We need to be prepared to have prices changed often (daily and perhaps
even hourly at the peak of the inflation). The service-

oriented businesses, such as retail stores where the prices - aided by today's computers - can be changed almost continuously, would be more desirable than say an educational service where the entire fee would be received at the beginning of a course. The only solution for this latter case would be if the money, when received, could be invested in something that would keep ahead of the rampant inflation.

INVESTMENTS FOR A DEPRESSION

In many ways we have to change our thinking concerning investments and depressions. If we were going to have inflation and followed by a *traditional* deflationary depression, we would want our investments during the inflationary period to be in things such as gold and silver that would keep ahead of inflation; as the depression began, we would want to liquidate those and be all in cash or bonds, so that as prices fell we could buy real estate and other items at bargain basement prices. Many investment advisors and economists are advocating this type of mentality. I simply do not think that it is going to work this time, since the inflation is going to continue throughout much, if not all, of the depression. Thus, we must *remain* in investments that will keep ahead of the inflationary spiral.

The question then becomes, "Where does it all end?" At some point the money will become so worthless that there will have to be fiscal and monetary reforms. It would do no good to simply come out with a new currency and continue to print fiat, unbacked, paper money, because the new currency would soon become worthless also. Along with the new currency, we would have to have some significant fiscal reforms in the government, the very least of which would be to balance the federal and local budgets. This whole subject of a new monetary system, which includes the problem of the national debt, is too vast to even broach here.

The important point here is that at some point after the

money has become quite worthless (once or twice), there will be a new monetary system. That is so far away that we are not yet able to tell what might be a good strategy as one bridges the gap from one system to the next, but we will advise you well ahead of time. One thing is certain: one does not want to be in bonds of any kind or in anything denominated in a fixed amount of dollars. We have said this over and over again, and yet many people still have much of their net worth in C.D.'s (certificates of deposits), savings accounts, bonds, and so forth. With inflation at 10% and growing, these people are losing purchasing power every day that they leave their money in these fixed U.S. dollar investments.

WAGE AND PRICE CONTROLS

We have been suggesting that wage and price controls are coming and have given detailed information on how to survive them. If you are a new subscriber, we would recommend getting MISL #140, "Price Controls Cause Shortages", and MISL #141, "Prospering During Price Controls" (available for a contribution of $7 for the 2 issues). In these issues we pointed out that wage and price controls always cause shortages. The reason for this is that they hold the supply flat or make it decline, since there is less profit incentive for production. On the other hand, this increases the demand by making the price artificially low. Invariably, when you are forcing the supply to decline and encouraging the demand to grow, shortages will occur.

If we have wage and price controls in 1979, shortages will occur in many items. Thus, I would encourage you to have an extra supply of anything that is essential for your business or your home. You can replenish this supply as you use it.

Other things we suggested in these articles were to go ahead now and raise prices substantially, *before* the wage and price controls occur, and then give discounts so that your prices are competitive. In the era of the wage and

price controls, you can simply reduce - ultimately to
zero - these discounts. There is much more we could say
about the wage and price control era, but this has been
covered in these two previous issues and we trust that
you will get them, or reread them if you already have
them.

Probably the wage and price controls will be on for about
12 to 18 months. When they are finally taken off, prices
will rise to a point higher than if the wage and price
controls had never been instituted in the first place.
Wages and prices, when artificially controlled, act much
like a leaf spring which, when held down and then released, tends to fly up not only to its normal position,
but to a position above what would have been "normal".
After the wage and price controls are removed, inflation
will hit us with a vengeance. We will have more to say
about inflation later in this article.

THE GOVERNMENT'S ANSWER WILL BE INDEXING

Indexing is a system whereby wages and prices and other
financial items (loans etc.) are geared to and connected
to a price index. In the U.S. this is the CPI (Consumer
Price Index). The way this works is that when something
is geared to the CPI, if the CPI goes up 1% a person's
wages or prices also go up 1%.

On pages 78-79 of the book, Bad Times & Beyond, published
by Dell Publishing Co., Inc., we read the following:
"BLS Commissioner Shiskin had hoped to gain the CPI
'national indicator' status. After all, a 1 percent increase in the CPI now triggers at least $1 billion in
additional wage, pension and Social Security payments
to almost 50 million persons, 88 percent of whom are paid
directly out of the public purse. When dependents are
taken into account, Shiskin recently wrote, the incomes
of 'somewhere in the neighborhood of one-half the population already are or soon will be pegged to the CPI.'"

As this points out, many of the pensioners, social security recipients, labor unions and so forth already have their salaries and incomes paid on a basis of the CPI. As this trend occurs more and more, and I would encourage you to get in on it now if you are employed; soon the economy will not be able to take this additional burden. At that time I'm afraid that some people, like those retired and living off of social security, will have their indexing removed. Woe unto you who become unindexed.

Indexing in countries like Brazil is also done on any long-term indebtedness. Thus, the principle is continually raised so that your monthly payments go up in exact proportion to the rise in the CPI.

Jimmy Carter has in effect just announced indexing for the United States. What he said was that if people will keep their wage increases to 7%, he wants the government to give them a tax rebate on any difference in that and the CPI. Thus, if inflation were at 15%, and a person's wages only went up 7%, the government would give them the 8% differential. If inflation hit say a 27% level, a person could be receiving a substantial amount from the government because of the 20% differential. Carter, in considering indexing, has accepted continued inflation.

Tying this subject of indexing to the superinflation that is going to occur after wages and prices are controlled and then decontrolled, people will scream and howl at the inflation and I believe that indexing will become a way of life in the U.S. Therefore, I would not provide funds for any long-term loans between now and the time that indexing is in full force and accepted by everyone. On the other hand, be sure that any loans on which you are on the receiving end are not indexed, do not have a variable interest rate clause, or anything of this nature. I believe that there will be a time, about 2 years from now when interest rates will be down to 6% again, when you can enter into long-term indebtedness and have a clean loan agreement. So bide your time, but be sure that there is no indexing involved in any of the small print, if you take out a loan.

Jim Sinclair, in his excellent newsletter (*James Sinclair & Company*, 55 Water St., New York, NY 10041) evaluated in this way Carter's proposal for tax relief of labor to be tied to the rate of inflation:

'''Indexation', a tactic utilized by countries who have capitulated to inflation (and therefore based on the assumption that inflation is here to stay), is a method of easing the burden of a particular economic sector. In this instance, it takes the form of a tax rebate or credit to maintain the buying power of labor union members, who perservered in their demands for wage increases to the suggested and astonishingly high level of 7%.

"To put into proper perspective what a 7% increase in wages, accompanied with a 7% rate of inflation, means, consider the following statistics, released by the administrators for the Social Security Trust Funds, which estimate the cost of living in the 21st Century:

ASSUMPTION OF ANNUAL INCREASE IN WAGES OF 5.75% AND IN PRICES OF 4%

The average worker retiring at age 65 would draw retirement checks of nearly $259,000, while some individuals would get the maximum of $405,000, the agency estimates.

If the Social Security projections hold true, wages will increase roughly 62-fold over the next 72 years. If prices followed suit:
__*Today's 60-cent loaf of bread would cost $37.50.*
__*A $25 tab at the grocery store would run $1,562.*
__*A 15-cent phone call or newspaper would cost $9.40.*
__*A medium-sized $4,500 auto would retail for $281,000.*
__*A $55,000 home would sell for $3.4 million.*
__*And that average $656,000 wage earner would be paying more than $50,000 annually in Social Security taxes. The maximum tax would be $114.000 on income up to $1.5 million.*

"Furthermore, this release stated that a typical collection of goods and services which cost $10 in 1967, cost $13,30 in 1973, $17 in 1976, and a shocking $19.80 this year.

"When President Carter's so-called 'strong measures' to combat inflation (containing an INDEXATION scheme) were announced, foreign exchange traders immediately offloaded Dollars. During the course of his speech, the Yen went from 181.50 per Dollar to 179, with the Swiss Franc and Deutsche Mark following suit. It was staggering to watch two screens simultaneously - one of President Carter speaking, and the other, the Reuters Money Wire, which displays all world banks, foreign exchanges and metals markets. As the anti-inflation message soared, the Dollar dived.

"The technique of indexation was coupled with a socialist approach. Labor was to be rewarded for cooperation while industry was threatened. The administration expressed its opposition to further tax relief. The trend towards STATE CAPITALISM, a form of socialism, was accelerated. Not surprisingly, the stock market continued its decline, gold climbed inexorably, and the Dollar suffered another round of humiliation.

"Those of us with Swiss Franc, Yen and Deutsche Mark denominated bonds, gold coins, and hard money of long term holding can rejoice at our profits, yet surely this celebration has funereal overtones, for the Father of our prosperity, Capitalism, is dying. The transition from Capitalism to State Capitalism, is the cause of your profits. When you make your multimillions, you can fly to Switzerland and buy the franchise for a hot dog stand.

Or, if you can obtain a Swiss work permit, you could work as a laborer for two weeks, and on your return to the U.S., use your earnings to purchase the World Trade Center. This exaggeration has a slight, sad ring of truth to it. Although naturally I am delighted with the profits my clients have reaped, I detest the cause for it."

Jim Sibbet in his October 26, 1978 issue of *Let's Talk
Silver & Gold* (61 South Lake Avenue, Pasadena, CA 91101),
had this to say about Carter's talk:

"But there was one big surprise which negates everything
else, and will cause inflation to go even higher. He
proposed that wage earners who limited their gross wages
to an annual increase of 7% would be rewarded with an income tax rebate of the difference between 7% and the
price inflation rate. This is called 'Indexation'.

"If the inflation rate remains at 10%, then a tax rebate
of 3% of the annual gross wages would be made. This will
have the effect of raising almost everyone's wages 7%
and guaranteeing a minimum floor inflation rate of 7%
even if the government's budget was in balance! But 3%
of the nation's gross payroll is an enormous amount.
This loss of tax revenue added on top of the present budget deficit will create the largest budget deficit in
history!

"Carter admitted that budget deficits were inflationary.
Thus instead of a 10% price inflation rate, his proposals
will stimulate a much higher rate. This in turn will
provide even greater tax rebates and even greater budget
deficits which will spiral upwards at an accelerating
rate.

"It will cause such a large rise in prices that the public will clamor for mandatory rent and price controls,
but continuing the tax rebate scheme. This leaves wages
plus tax rebates to rise at the same rate as the inflation price rate and effectively indexes wages with the
price inflation as is done in Brazil. With wages indexed and prices semi-controlled by tax penalties, you
can imagine the kind of profit squeeze that will take
place on corporate earnings. It will throw most corporations into a deficit.

"This will virtually eliminate the corporate income tax
because of no net income. Since corporations paid an

important part of total taxes last year, that amount
too will be added to the government's budget deficit
making it astronomical. . . .

"In conclusion, Pres. Carter has thus guaranteed a rapid
and large increase in the inflation rate and has done
nothing to support the Dollar. The Dollar's decline
should continue until more effective mandatory price controls are instituted a year or more hence (phase IV), but
before the next Presidential elections in Nov. 1980. By
then, mandatory price controls will be very popular with
the average ignorant voter because price inflation may
very well be at a 15%, maybe 20% rate by then, and will
be blamed on those businessmen not following the 5.75%
guideline.

"President Carter will undoubtedly be reelected because
his image will be that of the underdog inflation fighter
who is being defeated by the selfish and greedy businessmen. The lure of mandatory price controls with criminal
penalties and indexed wages (after experiencing 15%-20%
inflation) will be irresistible to the average ignorant
voter."

MORE AND MORE INFLATION

Inflation has become a way of life with us. However, it
is dangerous and you should be aware of its many pit-
falls. From pages 109-110 of the book, *Bad Times & Beyond*, we read: "'Inflation is dangerous because it creates a situation where price increases are considered
automatic. But as a distributor, I'm a middleman, and
if the factory wants to raise prices, it's OK with me
because I just pass them on to my customers. And no one
even questions the increases; they just expect them.
And the shortages in some ways are to our advantage because people aren't particular anymore. They'll take
what they can get.'
                    —Dick Arlington, 37, distributor of
                    oilfield instruments and owner of furni-
                    ture upholstery firm, Houston, Texas"

Inflation works solidly agianst the consumer, who is
faced with shortages, reduction in choices and rip-off.

Why do I think that there is going to be continuing inflation, even through a depression? I have answered that
question many times in various issues of the newsletter,
but let me summarize it in just a few sentences. As
long as the government deficit spends, they will have to
basically create money in the amount of the deficit.
This creation and passing out of money causes prices to
rise. The government is going to continue to operate in
the deficit.

If by Aristotelian and Boolean logic you analyze the
three premises stated above, the only conslusion that
you can come up with is that *there will be continued
inflation*. We have gone too far. It is just about impossible for the government to balance its budget. As
we pointed out in the last issue of MISL, right now during the business recovery part of the cycle, we should
be running a budget surplus in the federal government,
even according to Keynesian economists. However, we are
not, and it is estimated that the combined deficit for
1978-1979 will be approximately $118 billion. When we
go into a period of recession and the government really
fires up the spending mill, then what will the deficit
be?   It *could* be $100 billion per year!

The only way the government could solve its problem would
be to take many people off of welfare, unemployment and
other benefit programs, cancel government contracts, fire
government employees and raise taxes. I do not see much
evidence that the government is going to do any of these
four things with any sincerity. In a forthcoming issue
of MISL we will have more to say about the bankrupt condition of the federal government, and why it is almost
inevitable at this point in history that it continues to
operate in ever-increasing deficits.

Inflation is now at 10% and growing, and I believe that
we will see it above 15% by the end of 1979. The re-

cent accelerated crash of the U.S. dollar will have an
incredible impact on prices in the U.S. Not only are
the prices of all imported goods increasing, but also
the prices of all the basic commodities, which have a
worldwide price. The price of steel, wheat, cotton and
so forth will rise because the other currencies can buy
more of them for the same amount of currency - Swiss
francs, Deutsche marks or Japanese yen. As the price of
wheat goes up, so does the price of bread. As the
price of cotton goes up, so does the price of clothes.
As the price of steel goes up, so does the price of automobiles, refrigerators and so forth. Before the full impact of this dollar devaluation is felt, we will probably
see the inflation rate at 20% or above.

I'm not sure at what point the government will institute
wage and price controls, but certainly by the time inflation hits 20%. With the government interfering in the
economy, not only will there be wage and price controls,
but they will also be continually raising the discount
rate to fight inflation, and at some point they are going
to throw us into a recession. If the government is willing to let inflation go wild, they could forestall the
recession until after the 1980 elections. The Carter administration is definitely afraid of a recession, and
much less concerned about inflation. However, in order
to forestall the inevitable recession, they would probably
have to let the inflation rate get above 20%. Since I do
not believe that this is tenable to them, at some point
think there will be wage and price controls and an attempt to at least level things off until they can get reelected.

It is really a race to the wire to see which is going to
occur first: the 1980 elections, a significant recession, or 20% inflation.

SUMMARY AND CONCLUSION

We have looked at inflation and the fact that it will
continue to be with us in ever-increasing magnitude, even

throughout a depression, until a totally new monetary system is imposed upon us. During the depression, one must factor continued rising prices into one's strategy.

In long-range preparation for that depression, people need to consider their vocation, business, residence and investment situation, and make moves accordingly. For the short-term outlook, we see significantly higher inflation next year, and therefore would encourage our readers to buy significant capital items now, before there is a substantial increase in their price. Anything big that is needed for next year should be purchased during 1978.

5

Be Prepared for
WAGE AND PRICE CONTROLS

Reprinted from MISL #198, December 1979

In our judgment there is a good chance that we will see
wage and price controls imposed upon the U.S. economy
next year. We will have more to say about our other projections for 1980 in the next issue.

Preparing for wage and price controls takes some time,
effort and, in many cases, rearranging of one's affairs.
This is why it seemed appropriate to write about these
controls approximately six months ahead of time to allow
you the time necessary to make proper preparation.

WHY WILL WAGE AND PRICE CONTROLS BE IMPOSED?

Even though inflation is running at an all-time high, the
American public seems to be accepting it. There are no
beef boycott marches, and people seem to have adjusted to
the higher gasoline and fuel costs.

However, the only thing that the Carter administration is
supposedly doing to fight higher prices is raising the

interest rates. To date, this raising of the interest
rates has not caused prices to abate at all. Since we
project more and worse inflation ahead, as the increase
in the price of oil begins to permeate goods at the retail level, then at some point in time the consumers are
going to begin to be upset over the continued higher
prices. An appropriate time to make this "upsetness"
visible would be in a prime election year.

Thus, we look for the spring to bring about some unrest
among the consumers because of higher prices. Carter at
that time will want to "do something", and our best guess
is that it will be wage and price controls. He will have
the perfect excuse because he can claim that the volun-
tary wage and price guidelines that he has been establishing have basically been ignored by industry and the
unions. Since for a short while the average person
cheers and applauds wage and price controls, Carter will
probably time the announcement so that it will help him
in his reelection activities. Thus, we would give about
an 80% probability of controls being imposed some time
during late 1980.

WHAT DO WAGE AND PRICE CONTROLS CREATE?

In addition to the temporary euphoria among the consumers,
which is a minor short-term result of wage and price controls, there are two major results:

1. shortages
2. black markets

In this article, we will primarily be discussing shortages. If you stop and think about it, price controls
really *must* create shortages. Let's say that you froze
the price of a pair of shoes at $20, while the price
wanted to rise to $30 or $40 or more. In so doing, you
are creating additional demand because, to the consumer,
the price of this pair of shoes would be very cheap;
therefore, more people would want them. While increasing the demand, you are simultaneously decreasing the

supply because there is less profit incentive to make that pair of shoes, particularly as the cost of producing them begins to climb and approach $18 or $19. Thus, by the simplest of economic reasoning, when the demand for a product is increased and the supply is decreased, then shortages in that product are going to result.

In 1977 we had a severe winter with natural gas shortages in the East. Schools were closed because of lack of heat. People were shivering, and some even froze to death. The reason that we had the natural gas shortage was that the government had fixed a price ceiling on natural gas. Because of this, more and more buildings were being built that utilized natural gas for heating, because it was cheap. Since prices (and, therefore, profits) could not increase, there was less and less incentive to drill for natural gas and to ship it through the pipelines to the Northeast. The government, in trying to appease the crowds in the grandstands with low prices, actually created this shortage by the imposition of price controls.

Similarly, the United States is the only country in the world with gasoline lines and gasoline shortages. The reason is that the government is artificially keeping the price low by price controls. In other countries a gallon of gasoline is $2 and in some cases even $3.

Thus, we see another principle: if there is a scarce resource that is in demand, there are basically only three ways to allocate it:

1. Allow the price to rise to the point such that the demand decreases to equal the supply.
2. Queuing (standing in line for your turn to get the scarce resource) with an artificially imposed low price.
3. Rationing.

All of the other countries in the world have chosen the first, and I think the best approach to the gasoline

shortage. They have allowed the price to rise to the
point at which there was enough demand, but not too much.

In this kind of situation, if the price gets too high,
people will stop using the scarce resource to the degree
that an excess supply develops. Then the price will come
down a bit to the level at which the free market will determine that the supply and demand are equal (in balance).

The United States, on many occasions, has chosen the second route. For some reason it believes that people
would rather either stand in line or do without a product, rather than pay a higher price for it. The trouble
is that this has never worked successfully anywhere. You
can probably recall that many years ago, on television we
saw farmers killing baby chicks, or killing cattle and
letting them lie on the range. The reason for this was
that the government had controlled the price for which
the farmer could sell his chickens, but had not controlled the price of the grains that he had to buy to
feed the chickens. When it began to cost more to purchase the feed for the chickens than he could sell the
chickens for, the farmer had no choice but to dispose of
the baby chickens and not raise them to maturity. If he
had raised them and lost money on each one, it would have
been a sure road to bankruptcy for him.

This brings us to another problem - that of partial wage
and price controls. In this event, the wages of people
in larger companies are controlled, while those of people
in very small companies are not. This means that the
prices of certain things, such as chickens and beef are
controlled, while the worldwide commodity markets of
corn, wheat, soybeans and so forth are not controlled.
This makes the shortage situation even worse.

The only way that wage and price controls could have a
prayer of a chance of working, would be the way that it
is done in Russia, where they have total wage and price
controls on everything. Since partial wage and price
controls are a disaster, some President, somewhere along

the line, is going to try total wage and price controls.
If this comes about, it is going to have an incredible
impact on the commodity markets. I do not think that the
price controls coming next year will be total, so we will
not cover that aspect in this article.

HOW YOU CAN PROFIT FROM THE COMING PRICE CONTROLS

This is the title of a book by a friend of mine, Dr. Gary
North. I would highly recommend it. You can purchase it
by sending $10.00 to:

    North Loopholes
    P.O. Box 1580
    Springfield, Virginia 22151

Another view of price controls is that they create a redistribution of the wealth. Obviously you want to be on
the receiving end, not the giving end, of that redistribution. Dr. North, in his book, describes it this way:
". . . the official prices are fictitious. Fewer transactions, proportionate to total transactions, take place
at the official prices. Prices are not controlled by the
authorities, for that is not possible; only *visible monetary prices* are controlled. Even more accurately, those
people who are forced to sell at official monetary prices
and those who would be willing to buy at higher prices,
but who cannot locate legal sellers, are controlled.

"Price controls therefore involve a *redistribution of
wealth. First,* some people are compelled to sell at
prices lower than they would otherwise have preferred to
receive and would have been able to receive. The beneficiaries are, of course, the buyers. The intended beneficiary is the 'little guy.' The actual beneficiaries -
legal beneficiaries - are the Federal government, the
higher officials in various governments, and those people
who are willing and able to stand in long lines for many
hours (and whose alternative uses of their time are, in
their estimation, less valuable than the goods they receive). *Second,* wealth is transferred to those who pro-

duce goods and services favored by the government, or
those who produce goods produced in the uncontrolled seg-
ments of the economy ('luxuries'), assuming that these
producers would not have prospered so well under conditions of open competition and free pricing. The losers
are, of course, producers who would have profited under
the free market and those consumers who would have bought
from them. *Third,* wealth is transferred to those who
have fewer moral qualms or fears about participating on
the illegal markets, since available goods and services
tend to flow in the direction of these markets. The larger the discrepancy between the legal monetary price of a
good and the monetary inflation-induced illegal market
price, the more goods are transferred to the alternative
markets. The losers are the morally inhibited, or fear-
inhibited, or information-lacking, or barterable re-
source-lacking citizens. Above all, the losers are the
propaganda-manipulated patriotic citizens. Under all
price control schemes, this law rules: *cynics win, pa-
triots lose.* That is the curse of government-controlled
prices. *Fourth,* repairmen win. *Fifth,* those who own
used goods win, since used goods are not controlled. *In
short,* those who possess the *real* money or monies win:
good looks, power, goods, inside information, barterable
skills, cynicism, and so forth."

TWO BASIC METHODS OF PRICE CONTROLS

We have been discussing the most common form of price
controls. This was the type used in World War II, the
Korean War and under Nixon. In this case, the government officially creates a maximum price for various
goods and services. The "jawboning" approach is simply a
version of this, where the government, by weight and mus-
cle, tries to get the various producing groups to adhere
to maximum prices, without them being officially decreed.

There is another form which does not appear to be price
control, but which is just as much a method of price control as the other. This is where the government says
that it will buy or sell a certain product at a fixed

price in unlimited quantity. The government has controlled the price of both gold and silver in this way in
times past. For many years the U.S. government said that
it would buy or sell gold at $35.00 an ounce in unlimited
quantities. Thus, it controlled the price at $35.00 and
could continue to control it in this manner until its resources were depleted.

In either type of price control, once the controls are
removed, the price of the product or item tends to rise
to a price higher than where it would have been, had no
controls been imposed. This is what happened to the
price of gold during the years 1972, 1973 and 1974.
There was a huge upward movement to bring gold up to
where it would have been, had the U.S. government not re-
stricted it for many years with that form of price control. However, a price is like a pendulum. When the
control is lifted, it would tend to initially go up even
higher than what it should have been. Thus, during 1975
and 1976 we saw the retracement of the price of gold back
down to a level where it would probably have been, had
the government never imposed its price control.

TAKE ACTION THE DAY THE CONTROLS ARE IMPOSED

When price controls first go on, they are usually at the
current market price. The supply of the product flowing
from the producer to the consumer will continue "as is"
for a period of time before shortages begin to occur.
This brings us to one of McKeever's cardinal rules:

> *The day price controls are announced on a product,
> go out and buy all that you are going to need for
> a good while, while the supply is still available.*

For example, if an individual had purchased two new cars,
extra automobile tires, and so on, on December 8, 1941,
he would have made out very well. If you own a manufacturing company that requires ball bearings to produce a
finished product, then the day price controls are announced, go out and buy all the ball bearings that you
can get your hands on. You cannot afford to spend sever-

al days contemplating whether or not to make the purchases, and how you are going to make them. Place the
purchase orders and then do the worrying, while your orders are being filled. This principle applies to almost
any trade: if you are a contractor, buy nails; if you
are a doctor, buy that piece of replacement equipment
that you have been wanting; if you are a housewife, buy
ample supplies of soap, detergent, cleansers, canned food
and so forth, but do it immediately when price controls
are imposed, not several weeks later. By then shortages
may have already occurred.

PREPARING FOR PRICE CONTROLS

Most subscribers to MISL have items that they would consider to be their "inflation hedge". What we are now
contemplating is what we should have for our "price controls hedge". We need to be prepared for both eventuali-
ties. In fact, in my opinion, price controls are more
likely than a runaway inflation. The question then is,
"How can we be best prepared for controls and the shortages that will follow?" I would like to suggest the
following specific ways:

1. RENT: If you are presently renting, buy a place or
become good friends with your landlord. If you are a
landlord, convert to either luxury apartments or single
family dwellings. With rent controls, housing shortages
will occur. In Vancouver, B.C., where we used to live,
they have rent controls and there is a tremendous shortage of apartments. Most apartment houses have a waiting
list. One favorite ploy of the landlord to get around
the rent controls is to furnish a previously unfurnished
apartment with very cheap furniture. He can then rent it
for the "regulated price" and then charge an enormous
price to rent you the furniture. In some cases, people
want to move in their own furniture and the landlords are
then able to charge them a storage fee for the "furnished
furniture". Other ploys have been used, such as the
landlord suggesting that a prospective renter buy a
water-color painting done by his wife (at a handsome

price), before he will let the person rent an apartment. For the person doing the renting, long-term leases are some protection. Having good relations with your land- lord, and being the best tenant he has, will also help. However, it could be that the purchase of a home or con- dominium would insure a "fixed rent".

2. AUTOMOBILES: Prepare for gasoline shortages, parts shortages, and high repair bills. Whether it be from the imposition of general price controls, another Arab oil embargo or slow down, or part of President Carter's energy conservation program, there is more gasoline shortage ahead. It is highly likely that gasoline ra- tioning (with coupons) will be used. The unknown is whe- ther this will be based on driver's licenses or on auto- mobile registrations. If it is based on driver's licen- ses, you should be willing to help anyone that you know of who does not have a driver's license to get one (friends, elderly relatives, teenagers). This may mean paying for driving lessons or taking someone down to take the test, but I am sure that in return that person would be happy to give you any ration coupons that would come to him because he had a driver's license. If it is based on automobile registration, buying or keeping a couple of extra $100 cars would bring in additional gasoline.

It is important to make friends now with your local gas station operator. Occasionally take him and his crew something cool to drink, or some cookies that your wife has made. When they're not rushed, visit with them and get to know them. When they are lubricating your car, hang around but don't get in the way. It's also essen- tial to buy a siphon hose with a bulb (so you don't get gasoline in your mouth when siphoning). Also buy a lock- able gas cap. In a gasoline shortage these are two of the first items that will disappear. (Like emergency road flares, there aren't any available to buy when you need one.)

Dr. North, in referring to the shortages during World War II, had the following to say about the gasoline problem. He first quotes Frederic Andre: '''Perhaps the item whose

shortage most curtailed our normal living was the gasoline shortage. To cope with this, Dad secured both the
regular 'A' category of gas rationing coupons and also
the 'C' category (perhaps because he was entitled to it
as a minister). Anyway, when gasoline ran low, Dad
would somehow persuade a friendly farmer to direct the
hose of his 200-gallon farm vehicle tank into our car gas
tank and into miscellaneous gas cans in the trunk.'
(This 'farmer-supplied fuel' scheme is operating today in
the case of diesel fuel, since 'farm only' diesel fuel is
tax-free.) Even more devious, however, was the scheme
related by S.E. Barber: 'In the area of gasoline rationing I can't remember all the details, but the various
categories for civilian use were 'A, B, & C' (stamps
worth 3-5 gallons each) for autos, 'K' stamps for trucks,
'J' for utility, etc. The dodge lay in (1) plant a 'vic-
tory garden' (officially sanctioned by Fed-Gov); (2) buy
some form of power equipment (rototiller, small tractor,
etc.) - even if it *doesn't* run, you've *still* got a model
number and serial number - and apply at local ration
board for gas stamps to run the thing. Garden by hand
and use the 'J' stamp gas in your car'. . .

"Gasoline rationing was the biggest bureaucratic problem
for the OPA. There were too many cheaters. Everyone
knew there were ample supplies of gasoline (the controls
had been imposed to reduce the consumption of rubber by
tire users), and Americans, then as now, wanted to use
their cars. The OPA bureaucrats tried to give some
groups special treatment because of their special needs
(ministers and physicians), but everyone wanted prefer-
ential treatment some of the time. So the evaders went
to work. First, there were millions and millions of
counterfeits. The ration coupons were really money, so
they were treated as such by private printers. The
'money' was less familiar to gas station attendants, so
they could be passed fairly easy. But the gas station
owners became buyers of counterfeits. They would sell
gasoline to buyers who didn't have ration coupons; then
the station owners would turn in the counterfeits that
they had bought. If they were caught (which was seldom
until after the war), they could always plead ignorance.

'Some shady gasoline buyers just fooled me, your honor.' Chester Bowles testified before Congress that the profits were a billion dollars a month in 1944 (I think Chet's days as a big-time advertising man may have gotten the better of him). Profits were there, certainly, and the risks really were minimal. While surveys of stations by OPA enforcers indicated that 60% of them were participating to some extent in illegal sales, only 15,094 sanctions were imposed throughout the war. Yet there had been 250,000 stations in 1941. Only 3,500 of these were actually brought to court under criminal sanctions. In 1944, there were 124,000 cases revealing violations; sanctions were imposed in 8,700 cases. Risk? Not much. And everyone know it."

In addition to the gasoline problem, there will be a problem with shortages of parts and high repair bills. It would therefore be advisable, the day price controls are imposed, to be sure that you have, AT A MINIMUM, the following:

1. Tool kit (including spark plug wrench)
2. Distributor cap, points, condensers, rotor and coil
3. Fan belts
4. Spark plugs
5. Radiator and heater hoses
6. Windshield wipers
7. Oil, brake fluid and transmission fluid
8. Other spare parts, depending on the age of your car, such as fuel pump, brake cylinders, water pump, thermostat
9. Extra bulbs and fuses
10. Generator and starter brushes
11. Valve stems, and tire repair kit

It may be that you will not know how to install some of these parts, but it is good to have the parts so that someone who does know how can install them. If you are concerned about repair bills, learn to do some of the minor repairs yourself. (Anyone should be able to change spark plugs, for example.)

It would be good to have a small compact car that gets 40 to 50 miles per gallon. In some situations, families might even want to consider motor bikes. (These would be especially handy for getting out of the city if all the freeways were clogged with abandoned vehicles.)

3. LEARN TO BARTER. Barter is coming back to your neighborhood and community. Most people are so accustomed to "purchasing" things in a store that a face to face negotiation for an item would be a frightening experience. If this is your case, I would encourage you to begin to attend swap meets, garage sales, and other places where this type of face to face negotiation goes on. For a real experience, try doing it without money. Take a couple cans of a good brand of peaches, for example, and go to a garage sale and see what you can trade them for. In Germany, during the price-control shortage economy after the war, they had "barter boards" all over. On these people posted things that they were willing to trade. A take off on the same idea would be a "barter ad paper". When bartering begins to become popular, you could publish for your community a little weekly paper (mimeographed) listing the items that people wanted to trade for something. You could charge a small fee for listing an item on your barter sheet. Another key to the barter system is going to be close personal relationships. These may be developed in churches, service clubs, in your neighborhood, or in your office. People will much more likely deal and barter with someone they know and trust. Get used to lending people a helping hand and doing nice things for them. This bread that you cast on the water could come back to you many fold, if you need a favor (like a gas rationing stamp) when times get tough.

If one is going to barter (with goods), this necessitates a storing up of barterable items. Various writers and thinkers have suggested things such as cans of cigarette tobacco, bottles of wine, nails, ammunition, and toilet paper. My suggestion is that you don't blindly follow their advice, but that you figure out for yourself what the people *you* know would really need, if most things began to be in short supply. It is ideal if the item is storable for long periods of time and is contained in small units. Then lay in a supply of this and of various other barter items. (Don't put all of your eggs in one basket.)

4. FOR THOSE WHO OWN THEIR OWN BUSINESS: Prepare now. This subject is covered quite well in Mark Skousen's book, *Playing the Price Controls Game*. You can purchase this book for $9.95 from:

> Arlington House
> 165 Huguenot Street
> New Rochelle, New York 10810

One thing to begin to initiate is paying people a salary plus a bonus. By establishing this principle now you may be able to keep good workers by increasing their bonuses when wages are frozen and the only way they can get a raise is to change jobs. Have higher prices now and give large discounts, so that when price freezes go on, the discounts can slowly be eliminated. Cooperate with others in your industry.

Dr. North reports this concerning the building industry: "*Building materials* are always a problem under controls. Marshall Tilden's comments are especially revealing; where there is a will, you may get away: 'As a general contractor primarily building custom homes, I experienced serious difficulties in obtaining metal building products at any price. Several contractors got together at a lun- cheon and decided to have a bi-monthly meeting for the purpose of exchanging ideas to circumvent price controls and keep in business. One of the methods was to bid gov- ernment jobs in order to obtain priorities for materials. We usually were able to buy under priority more material than was actually required for each priority job. Each of us stockpiled all critical material we were able to purchase through any source and then we used these stock- piles for exchange. I had a salesman travel through the Midwest states buying stucco netting from material sup- pliers a roll at a time. These rolls were accumulated

80

and then shipped to me. The same way with nails. These
materials were used for trading purposes and kept me in
business. In some cases we paid double the control
price. The fact that I was buying one or more projects
under priority made this possible.' In short, *priority
slips served as the real money supply in the construction industry.*"

PROFITING FROM PRICE CONTROLS

There is a way to actually profit from price controls.
Basically, it involves becoming a middle man, or a finder.
In businesses this may mean finding paper for a printing
concern,building materials for a construction company,
and so forth. Those companies will be willing to pay you
a fee to spend time going around locating the items that
are in short supply. This approach is outlined well in
Dr. North's book. He points out that the time to make
all the contacts necessary for this is well ahead of the
imposition of price controls.

Similarly, on a much smaller scale, you could do this
type of thing for your friends, relatives and neighbors.
Someone may need a good used lawnmower (since new ones
will be in very short supply). You could take the time
to check out various used lawnmowers and find the best
one. If you're the type of person who has a sharp eye,
good intelligence and time to burn, this type of activity
might be worth considering.

THE MORAL QUESTION

To the best of my knowledge, everything that we have suggested is legal now and should continue to be legal even
after price controls are imposed. However, it may come
to be that some item you, or a member of your family, may
need desperately will simply not be available in the legitimate markets. (This occurs because, in a controlled
and shortage economy, goods flow from the legal markets
to the black markets. Actually I prefer the term "free
market", "underground market", or "alternative market" to

the term black market.) The question then arises as to
whether or not you deal with this underground market.
That is a tough moral question and each person is going
to have to think it through for himself.

I would like to share with you a couple thoughts I have.
It may be that price controls are actually unconstitu-
tional. It may be that one could deal in these alternate
markets and still not be breaking the Constitution. What
really *is* the "law of the land" - is it the Constitution
or the bureaucratic decisions? In the first centuries of
Christianity, the law of the Roman Empire said that it
was illegal to believe in Jesus Christ. Those first century Christians chose to disobey the "law of the land"
rather than deny their faith, and they were willing to
die for it. Evidently there were commands from God that
they classified as higher than the "law of the land".
The Bible also says that if a man does not provide for
his own family, he is worse than an infidel. Is this
command lower or higher than the "law of the land"?

Just to be sure that you understand my position, I am not
advising to do anything illegal. There are various in-
terpretations of what is legal. That is why we have our
elaborate court system. The preparations you can make
now are completely legal. After controls are imposed and
shortages begin, you'll need to analyze which of your alternatives you feel are legal, and which are definitely
not. After analyzing that, act accordingly.

SUMMARY AND CONCLUSION

We have seen that inflation is going to continue. Prices
will continue to rise as the government prints and dis-
tributes more and more money. Rather than attacking the
root of the disease and balancing the federal budget, the
government will likely attack only the symptoms and im-
pose price controls as an attempt to control inflation.
I believe that the likelihood of the imposition of price
controls is very high.

In the government's well-meaning attempts to help us, it
inevitably hurts us. The imposition of price controls
will cause shortages. When certain items are in short
supply at legal prices, there will be an underground market where these can be purchased at prices much higher
than they would have been, had the government not imposed
the controls. To prepare for this price-controlled shortage economy, that we could well enter into within the
next couple of years, one needs to begin preparing now,
since many of the preparations will take months to
achieve.

Each person must evaluate the future for himself. All of
our decisions are based on our view of the future. If
your view of the future involves, as mine does, a good
likelihood of price controls, then evaluate now what preparations need to be made. And remember, planning without taking action is useless, so *plan your actions and
act your plan*. Begin to acquire your PRICE CONTROLS
HEDGE.

6

Be Prepared for

A BANKING CRISIS

There are many people today, of whom I am one, who are concerned that we are going to have a banking crisis in America in the not-too-distant future. This banking crisis could potentially be far worse than the banking crisis of 1931-1932.

Shortly after the banking crisis of 1931-1932, Americans were very skeptical about depositing money in a bank. They spent a great deal of time checking out a bank to be sure that it was a safe one. To find a reliable bank in those days was a difficult task.

Today, most depositors don't seem concerned at all about how solvent and solid their banks are. They blindly trust the bankers and the government regulators to take care of everything. That thought alone should cause concern in any thinking depositor.

WHAT COULD POSSIBLY BE WRONG WITH OUR BANKING SYSTEM?

There are so many things that are wrong with our banking system that it is difficult to even begin to des-
cribe them all. In the first place, even by our own
government standards (which we will see later are in-
adequate) only about 66 percent of all the banks in
the United States are listed as even "satisfactory."
Their loan-to-deposit ratios are way out of line.
They are carrying bad debts on their books. They are
carrying assets on their books at far more than their
true values. They are borrowing short and loaning
long. They are reliant upon foreign deposits, and the
list of problems could go on and on.

Let's look at these weaknesses one at a time and try
to help you evaluate your own bank. Then we will discuss some of the things you could do to potentially
protect yourself against the coming banking crisis.

THE U.S. METHOD OF ACCOUNTING

As most businessmen know, the U.S. government requires
a different method of accounting than most of the rest
of the world. On a business financial statement you
can list only what you paid for an item as its present
value. To take a ridiculous example, if you had a rich
uncle who sold you a 50-story office building for one
dollar, you could never show that asset as worth more
than one dollar on your financial statement, regardless
of its market value.

However, when this is applied to the banking environment, it tends to work in a way that actually deceives
the public. For example, if a bank bought stock in a
company for, perhaps, $1,000,000, and the value of the
stock kept dropping and dropping until it was worth
only $200,000 in the stock market, the bank would still
show that as a $1,000,000 dollar asset. Similarly, if
the bank bought bonds, and they had an incredible fall
in value as they did in 1979 and 1980, the bank would

still carry them at the higher value of what they paid
for them rather than showing them as an asset at what
they were actually worth.

In Europe, most governments require the banks to re-
value all of their assets at current market values
every six months. Thus, if you were to look at the
financial statement of a European bank, the bank statement will reflect the true market value of the assets.
This is realistic accounting, but our government requires U.S. banks to do what I call "fantasy" accounting.

BAD LOANS STILL CARRIED AS ASSETS

For businesses, the government requires that bad loans
and bad debts be written off. They cannot be carried
as assets of a company. Banks should be required to
do the same thing, but they are not.

Some of our major banks have loaned out billions on
real estate trusts (REIT's), to less-developed countries (LDC's), and to countries behind the Iron Cur-
tain. Many of these loans are just plain bad loans
and will never be repaid.

In Europe, most banks would consider a loan bad when
the borrower (whether it is a foreign government or
not) could no longer repay part of the principal when
it was due. They certainly would consider it bad when
the borrower could not pay the interest but had to
borrow additional funds to pay the interest. Many
loans made by U.S. banks are in exactly this condition:
the borrowers cannot even pay the interest due. Yet
the banks continue to carry them on their books as
good loans. That's incredible.

Donald Hoppe, in his excellent newsletter (P.O. Box
513, Crystal Lake, IL 60014) had this to say about
these LDC loans in a recent issue:

"Events are now moving so swiftly that a major breakdown in the world's economic and financial structure
should be anticipated within the next two years. Unfortunately, because of the unprecedented deteriora-
tion in world financial and monetary conditions over
the past ten years, and because of the incredible de-
pendency of the leading industrial nations on OPEC
oil, the exact nature of this breakdown cannot be predicted at this time. All that can be said for sure is,
(1) that things cannot go on much longer as they are,
and (2) that no one in authority appears to have any
idea of how financial equilibrium and international
monetary stability can be restored.

"During the past decade, some of the largest U.S. banks
became multinational corporations that now derive as
much as 50 percent of their income from foreign lending, particularly to the less developed countries
(LDC's). As a result of chronic U.S. balance of payment deficits and the activity of private American
banks overseas, a new source of international capital,
the so-called 'eurodollar' market has developed. This
market has not only grown to enormous size (now estimated at $250 billion), but is entirely unregulated
and unmonitored. Furthermore, the lending and relend-
ing of these funds has become so complex and so intri-
cate that it would be impossible to predict the beha-
vior of this market during a severe world financial
crisis.

"The quadrupling of world oil prices by the OPEC cartel
in 1973 brought the international credit situation,
which had already been deteriorating for years, to the
critical stage. Almost overnight, private multinational banks became the primary source of credit for those
countries experiencing severe balance of payments
deficits as a result of oil imports. By the end of
1976 these banks had more than $300 billion in loans
outstanding. The public external debt of the LDC's
alone is estimated at between $150 and $200 billion,
with at least $50 billion owed to U.S. private banks
and another $25 billion or so to European banks.

"Typically, the LDC's are now spending about 20 percent of their export earnings just to pay interest on their debts. And in the financially weakest of these countries, such as Brazil, Zaire, Turkey and Mexico, interest payments alone can consume more than 40 percent of external income. Most of the LDC loans are short term. The seriousness of the international debt problem may be judged by the fact that it involves amounts so large that they cannot even be estimated within $50 billion! Furthermore, it is almost openly acknowledged in government and banking circles that there is no real hope that many of the LDC's will *ever* be able to repay the principal of their outstanding loans, and some are now having great difficulty even meeting their interest payments.

"The really horrendous part of this problem is that the need of the LDC's for credit is now greater than ever, because of still higher oil prices and because of a general price weakness in many of the commodities that are their primary source of income. Consequently, the banks must continue to lend new funds to the LDC's, because to do otherwise would bring about an open default of existing loans and cause the international banking collapse and panic they are so desperately trying to avoid.

"Most government efforts in this area are aimed at devising a plan to allow the private banks to continue lending, with some sort of 'official' guarantee of repayment from the IMF or other international agency. But this too might well cause more problems than it solves. Any direct attempt to create new financial assets out of nothing on a scale that would be required to bail out, not only the LDC's, but the majority of the advanced nations (that are also being economically strangled by mounting national and international debt) could,and very likely would, result in a panic flight from paper currencies, leading to a worldwide hyperinflation and financial collapse.

"Thus we are poised between a massive international debt default and banking crisis, which would obviously be drastically deflationary and result in a severe world depression, and an IMF or central bank rescue attempt, which would introduce an enormous new expansion of credit and almost certainly result in a highly destructive escalation of inflation.

"Although it might now appear to the industrial nations that they have no choice but to rescue both their own banks and the LDC's with some new fiat credit creation, regardless of the inflationary consequences, they would accomplish nothing by doing so - except the final destruction of their fiat currency and credit systems. It should be obvious that the price of OPEC oil would simply be increased to discount the reduced value of any unwarranted expansion in the number of existing monetary units, leaving the oil importing countries in worse shape than before."

It is a known fact that some of the major U.S. banks have loaned millions to the nation of Panama. Panama was ready to default on these loans which could have caused a banking crisis at that time. Much of the big push and pressure to get the Panama Canal reverted back to the Republic of Panama *and* to give them many millions in payments in addition to the canal is thought by many to have been engineered by the major banks so they could get their loans repaid.

We could look at many other poor practices such as banks loaning money against insurance policies which ultimately turned out to be fraudulent, and loaning money against real estate which is today worth a fraction of the value of the loans.

If many of the major banks in the United States were to come up with true and accurate financial statements, stating their assets at current market values and writing off all bad loans, many of them would have to declare bankruptcy. Government regulators, with the charter to keep the banks solvent, are doing this, but it is really a paper exercise. If they were operating under Swiss banking regulations, the truth would come out, and many of them would be out of business.

FOREIGN DEPOSITS

Foreign deposits are placed in many of the major U.S. banks usually on a short-term basis. Of the four biggest banks in the United States, foreign deposits as a percentage of all deposits range from Bank of America with 38 percent of its deposits being foreign deposits to Citicorp with 53 percent. Much of these foreign funds have come from the depositing of petro-dollars of the OPEC countries (we'll have more to say about these petro-dollars in a moment).

Unfortunately, even though many of these foreign deposits can be withdrawn within 30 days, the banks are loaning these funds out for much longer periods of time, in some cases even years (called borrowing short and lending long). Banks should operate in exactly the opposite way. They should borrow money on a long-term basis and lend it out on a short-term basis to be healthy, solvent banks. Of course if these foreign depositors (or even U.S. depositors) were to all demand their money, the banks simply could not pay because they have loaned out, in many cases, more than 100 percent of the deposits.

LOAN OUT MORE THAN 100 PERCENT?

You may say, "More than 100 percent - that's impossible." Not with our fractional banking system. Let's say that someone deposits $100,000 at a bank. The Federal Reserve requires the bank to keep a certain percentage, let's just say 10 percent, as a reserve, and they can loan out the other 90 percent or $90,000. They loan that to someone who deposits the $90,000 back in the bank. The bank then must keep $9,000 in reserve and can loan out $81,000 of this $90,000 deposit. Whoever they loan the $81,000 to might deposit that in the same bank. They would have to keep $8,100 in reserve and could loan out the difference. This could go on and on. They could actually loan out 200 or 300 percent of that initial $100,000 deposit!

LOAN/DEPOSIT RATIO

This is a key number for a bank. This tells what percentage of the total deposits they have out in loans. In the five largest banks in the United States, this averages over 70 percent. I have seen smaller banks go as high as 125 percent or more.

Also, the type of loans that the banks have made are of great importance. If these loans were in long-term mortgages, a bank would have little chance of paying off if everyone wanted his money. On the other hand, if the bank has placed the funds in 30 and 90 day short-term loans, then the bank could very quickly pay off all its depositors.

PETRO-DOLLAR RECYCLING

While the ten-fold increase in the price of oil has created some financial crises for oil importing nations, it has really been a boon to the international banking industry. The massive excess from these OPEC countries has provided the major international banks with a vast new resource of deposits.

It is this huge influx of deposits that has prevented the U.S. from having a banking crisis in the past. These came in about the time that many of the LDC loans were going bad and the REIT loans were proving to be disastrous.

However, now our international banks are totally dependent on these foreign petro-dollars for their survival. What happens if there is another international crisis and the OPEC nations decide not only to cut off our oil but also to pull all of their petro-dollars out of our banks? The whole thing could come tumbling down like a house of cards.

HOW SAFE IS YOUR BANK?

It is one thing to be concerned about the big banks in the nation's banking system. Your primary concern as an individual, however, needs to be the status of the bank in which you have your own personal funds. There are a number of things that any wise and prudent depositor should consider doing:

1. Check carefully the financial statement of your bank. If you do not have the capability of doing this, take it to your accountant or auditor and let him evaluate it. Ask the bank for the national averages on things such as loan-to-deposit ratios, and find out if your bank is better or worse than the national average. Also, inquire about the nature of the loans it makes - if they are long-term or short-term and what security backs up these loans.

2. Keep only a small amount of funds in a bank. The remainder of your funds should be invested in *something*, even if it is U.S. Treasury bills (you lose money there because of inflation but at least there is security). Do not buy CD's because they are not covered by the FDIC.

3. Have an amount in cash (actual currency) equivalent to about three months of expenses.

4. Consider Swiss banks. The main one we recommend is:

> Hans Weber
> Foreign Commerce Bank
> Bellariastrasse 82
> 8038 Zurich Switzerland

5. Consider moving your account to a small bank rather than a large one. Most smaller banks have not made loans to foreign countries. Most of their loans are within their own community and the loans are much more sound.

I am sure you can think of many other things you might want to do to be sure that if the banking house of cards begins to topple, you will lose a maximum of 5 percent of your assets.

BANKS WALK THE PLANKS

R.E. McMasters, in a recent issue of his newsletter *The Reaper* (P.O. Box 39026, Phoenix, AZ 85069) had this to say:

"In the tradition of the days of scallawags and pirates, the banking industry may be about to walk the plank and take a deep plunge. Some of the statistics which follow will amply reveal that bankers have already plunged by making excessive loans. They may be about to find out that they were all wet in doing so.

"Seldom will anyone take broadside shots at the sacrosanct banking community. It must be the fog which surrounds them obscures the aim. Nevertheless, at the risk of a near miss, it must be said that most bankers know as much about money as you and I know about building prairie schooners. For example, during a recent banking convention in Montana which occurred during this summer's dollar panic in Europe, the topic of discussion was how to keep the savings and loans and credit unions from getting too many deposits. Can you imagine it? The bankers' only commodity, money (the dollar), under attack in Europe, with the potential of collapse and the bankers are sitting around talking about the trouble that the savings and loans and credit unions are giving them. That's akin to camping on a Colorado canyon floor with a flash flood bearing down, refusing to leave the tent because the raincoat can't be found. It shows not only a lack of ordered priorities, but also blatant ignorance.

"Recently, Mr. Robert E. Wieczorowski, former Director of the World Bank, told Conrad Jules Braun, of Gold Standard Corporation, that monetary events of the past few years had led him to conclude the harbingers of gold are correct. Question. What took Mr. Wieczorowski so long to come to this conclusion? After all, *he is Director* of the World Bank. Most bankers, sadly, are simply bureaucrats 'following the numbers' on a day-to-day basis. We, you and I, trust them. The evidence of our trust? Our demand deposit accounts!

"The American banking system is as vulnerable today as it was in the early 1930's. Let's look at some numbers. Only 66% of the banks in this country are in 'satisfactory' condition according to the Federal Reserve. One third are having payment problems. The banking industry's illiquidity peaked in 1974 at 72.3%. They were loaned up to the tune of 72.3%. That peak was exceeded in September of 1978 when the banks' illiquidity soared to 72.4%. The October issue of *The Bank Credit Analyst* concluded, 'The basic cyclical indicators are continuing to signal that the general credit environment is deteriorating.' Please recall that the last time (73-74) the banking industry faced a liquidity crisis, Franklin National Bank failed. Its demise almost toppled the banking system and came within a gnat's eyelash of triggering a run on the banks.

"It is assumed that the FDIC and the FSLIC will be able to guarantee all deposits against default in the case of a banking crisis. It is important to remember that both the FDIC and the FSLIC are government corporations, begun in 1933 & 1947, respectively. They do not have the reserves necessary to cover a banking failure (FDIC-$10 billion to back up $625 billion in deposits). Most folks take for granted the Federal Reserve will automatically print the money to back up the FDIC and FSLIC. In the '30's, however, the Federal

Reserve did not save some of its own member banks.
And, in any case, the SOP (Standard Operating Procedure) of both the FDIC and the FSLIC is to *transfer*
customer accounts from a defunct institution to a solvent one, *not* to pay out money to depositors.

"Banks need more deposits and/or paid off loans to increase their liquidity. Rubbing salt in the wound,
however, is the fact that U.S. banks are suffering from
a *drop* in OPEC investments, from $3.8 billion to $500
million in less than a year. Also, according to the
Federal Reserve Bank of St. Louis, during the second
quarter of 1978 foreign official holdings of U.S. assets declined by about $5 billion. To make matters
even worse, foreigners hold 25% of the $475 billion of
U.S. Treasury debt. Interest rates have to stay high
to keep these deposits 'on stream.' A withdrawal of
these deposits would force an incredible monetization
of the debt and result in a new dollar crisis that
would make our eyes water. The economy is slowing
down. The 'natural' result is for interest rates to
fall. However, they must be kept high enough to permit
a real return after inflation. It's like being between a rock and a hard place. But, really, it's a
damned if you do, damned if you don't situation. And
don't expect Nancy Teeters, the *liberal* economist who
was recently appointed to the Federal Reserve Board,
to have any miracle answers. The Fed's decision to
raise the discount rate half a point to a record $8\frac{1}{2}\%$,
highlighted the seriousness of the crisis.

"Here are some other cheery statistics:
  1. The loan to deposit ratio is not only higher
than the 1974 peak, but the highest it has been since
1920!
  2. Some of the *big* banks' loans aren't exactly
sterling booty. All those old "forgotten" REIT loans,
the oil tanker loans and the 'lesser developed country'
loans are still on the books.
  3. Weaker businesses have been borrowing to beat
the band.

4. Europeans hold 500-700 billion Eurodollars.
5. And the Arabs? Saudi Arabia alone holds $50 billion in U.S. Treasury notes.
6. Some $50 billion are loaned to behind-the-Iron-Curtain-Countries.
7. Business' liquidity is worse now than during the 1974 recession. In other words, business' cash situation has not improved during the three good years of this business cycle.
8. The consumer's saving rate is the lowest it has been in fourteen years.
9. The ratio of consumer debt to disposable after-tax personal income is close to an all-time high.
10. Ninety percent of all big ticket items purchased today by the consumer are on credit. In short, it looks as though the plank has about run out for the banks."

SUMMARY AND CONCLUSION

We have seen that our banking system is at best marginally "satisfactory" and at worst could be on the verge of collapse. This condition has been brought about by assets being overstated at their original cost value rather than market value, and many of the major banks carrying bad loans from LDC's, REIT's, and so forth, as good on their financial statements. It is further complicated by the major banks' heavy reliance upon foreign deposits, particularly the petro-dollars.

All these factors could cause a major international banking crisis at some point in the future. If the government doesn't move quickly enough, the system could collapse and banks fold. If the government does move quickly enough, they will simply pump in currency (or government checks) which will create an incredible hyperinflation.

There are things an individual depositor can do to be sure of the solvency and the soundness of his own

individual bank. He can arrange his financial affairs
so that he minimizes any loss from such a banking
crisis. He can do such practical things as have a
certain amount of actual currency in hand and some
amount of money in banks overseas (such as a Swiss
bank). If a person is aware ahead of time of what is
coming, he can take the appropriate actions to mini-
mize the impact of such a banking crisis on his financial life.

7

Be Prepared for

FOREIGN EXCHANGE CONTROLS

In many of these articles in this How-To-Be-Prepared series, it is intuitively obvious to the reader that any number of potential crises could endanger his financial or physical well-being. However, when we begin discussing foreign exchange controls, that danger is not readily apparent to the average reader.

In fact, most people are not quite sure what foreign exchange controls are or how such controls could affect them and their families.

WHAT ARE FOREIGN EXCHANGE CONTROLS?

When a country gets into financial difficulty, it begins to take a number of drastic measures. One of the measures that it usually takes is to limit (by taxation or quota) the import of certain raw goods or manufactured goods, thus interfering with the free market in an attempt to protect jobs or outmoded industries in the country.

What is really happening is the Balance of Trade (BOT) is continually going deficit. That means that they are buying from foreign countries much more goods and services than they are selling to the other countries. Thus, in composit, they continually have to pay out more than they are taking in in income, based on world trade.

An even bigger problem that these countries usually face is with their Balance of Payment (BOP). The balance of payment includes all financial transactions, not just those from commercial trade. Thus, the BOT is simply a portion of the BOP. In watching a country and its status in the world financial situation, the BOP is the key item to watch, not the BOT. They could be breaking even on their BOT but if many of their citizens are moving funds out of their country over to foreign banks, then this would cause their BOP to be in deficit or, in other words, much more capital would be flowing out of their country than is coming in.

Flight of capital out of a country can occur for a number of reasons. When a country's currency becomes shaky, or the citizens perceive it as being highly in- flated in relation to other currencies, they will move their money out of that country. Also, in former times when we had fixed exchange rates, just when a country was about to devalue its currency, the wealthier citi- zens would move their money out of that country into another currency and then, after the devaluation, bring it back in for a substantial profit. We also see flight of capital out of a country if it looks as if that country is going to reach its demise. We saw enormous flight of capital out of South Viet Nam for a year or two before its fall.

When countries sense a flight of capital out of their countries, which makes their BOP even worse, they tend to pass laws that say that no private citizen can move

funds out of their country, and they frequently curtail
the amount of funds that corporations can move out of
the country.

SO WHAT IF THERE ARE FOREIGN EXCHANGE CONTROLS?

After hearing the description of these foreign exchange
controls, perhaps the average reader of this book might
think: "So what? That wouldn't affect me." That
statement is both true and not true. It is true if one
intends to remain forever in the United States. By
"remain forever" I mean a decision is made not to
travel abroad, invest abroad, or move out of the United
States in the event that it becomes a dictatorship,
communistic, or some other undesirable form of government.

On the other hand, if an individual feels that he
should like to travel abroad or possibly move out of
the United States under certain circumstances, then
these foreign exchange controls could greatly affect
him.

This was brought home to me very vividly by a lady who
was in charge of our bookkeeping in a large consulting
firm I used to own. Her name is Tanya, and she came
from a very wealthy family in Cuba. Growing up, she
never made a bed, never ironed, never cleaned house or
washed dishes. All of the wealthy women in her family
sat around and embroidered and made beautiful things.
They had servants to do all of the menial housework.

Castro came in and took over Cuba, and her family,
being good loyal Cubans, remained there rather than
leave as some wealthy families did. As the regime of
Castro began to unfold itself, with all its brutality,
imprisonment and terrible economic chaos, life became
unbearable for Tanya and her family.

They applied for permission to leave Cuba, which Castro
granted. But he came into their home and inventoried

every item. They could take nothing with them. Thus, if a vase were broken, they had to keep the pieces to prove that they were taking nothing with them.

When Tanya landed in Florida, she had on a dress and over that two skirts and two blouses, and that was it. The rest of her family were similarly attired. They brought with them no money and no wealth. In a short 30-minute flight, they went from a great deal of wealth to abject poverty and were forced to live on this poverty level for many, many years.

I asked her one day why in the world her father didn't have a bank account with a fair amount of money in it in the United States, Switzerland, Mexico, Canada or someplace so that when they arrived in the United States they could have drawn on those funds and not had to live in poverty. Her reply was, "We didn't do it because we thought it could never happen in our country."

As I travel around and talk to Americans today, I find most of them have no fear of foreign exchange controls and have no inclination to have some of their wealth outside of the United States because, "It could never happen to our country."

Even rabbits and ground squirrels have a back door to their tunnels. It is unfortunate that human beings are not as intelligent.

WHEN DO YOU BUY INSURANCE?

You cannot buy fire insurance when your house is burning down. You cannot buy road flares when you need them. There are many things in life that must be bought ahead of time. Most of these fall into this broad category of "insurance." In this category I would also place things like fire extinguishers, road flares, automobile jacks, emergency flashlights, stored water, and even a Swiss bank account. These are all forms of insurance against emergencies.

Unfortunately, if one waits until he needs them, rarely
are they available. If you're caught out on the highway halfway between Los Angeles and Mojave and have a
flat tire and need a flashlight, a spare tire, or a
road flare, it's a long walk across the desert to be
able to buy one. Similarly, in thinking of moving
ten percent of one's assets to a Swiss bank (or a bank
in any other country), it will be possible but very
difficult after foreign exchange controls are insti-
gated by the government.

HOW TO OPEN A SWISS BANK ACCOUNT

A Swiss bank account can be opened today (the fall of
1980) very easily by mail. You can send a check
($5,000 is the minimum) to:

> Hans Weber, Managing Director
> Foreign Commerce Bank
> Bellariastrasse 82
> 8038 Zurich, Switzerland

Or you can send a check ($500 minimum) to:

> Banque Indiana
> P.O. Box 127
> 1001 Lausanne, Switzerland

You can ask either of these banks to open a "current
account" for you. They will deposit the money and
then send you the forms to sign.

For those who are concerned about financial privacy,
we have a recommendation for you. Of course the most
private way is to take actual cash to whatever bank in
whatever country you have chosen and deposit it personally. However, if you are doing it by mail, the
following procedure will help you maintain a great deal
of your privacy.

First, you cash a check at your own bank for whatever
amount you wish to deposit in Switzerland. Then you

go to another bank where you do not normally do business, and buy a cashier's check for that amount made out to yourself. On the back of this cashier's check you endorse it over to the bank. The reason for this is that the federal government requires banks to microfilm the *front* of these checks (but not the back). All that will then be passed under the microfilm camera of this bank (where you usually don't do business) is a cashier's check made out to yourself.

As of today, you can send over any amount. The banks are required to report anything that goes overseas in an amount more than $5,000. Thus, if you had a large amount to send over, to still maintain your privacy you could do it in multiple checks of $4,000 each.

If one lives near the Canadian or Mexican border of the United States, he could easily drive across the border and open an account in Canada or Mexico. The more private one can be in these transactions, the better, because it is possible that the government, with foreign exchange controls, could attempt to require its citizens to bring home any foreign deposits. This is less likely than not allowing any further movement of capital out of the United States, but it could happen.

WHAT IF I WAIT TOO LONG?

We always like to include this section in these articles on preparation because there are many people who do not believe in taking a stitch in time but would rather take nine later on. "Nine stitchers" can always get around the foreign exchange regulations if they have the time and money. One could take diamonds (which are not detected in airport metal detectors) of investment grade and rated by the AGI in a pocket or purse on a flight overseas. He could sell these diamonds overseas and do with the funds as he wished. One is likely to "take a beating" on the quick sale of these assets and perhaps some future law will even

make it illegal to take assets of any kind out of the
country (à la Cuba).

Many countries today will not allow their citizens to
take funds out of the country. One of these is
Australia. There is a businessman there who wanted
to take out $200,000 and the government would not let
him. He simply went down and bought a $200,000 yacht,
sailed it to Hong Kong, and sold it.

One can always buy something like a whole life insurance policy in the United States and then borrow
against that policy through a bank in a foreign country.

Some friends of mine went and lived in New Zealand for
a while. It was very easy to take all the money they
wanted into the country. However, when they started
to leave, the government blocked their bank account
and would not let them take anything out. In a situation like that, if they had withdrawn all their funds
from the bank and purchased portable but very valuable
assets, they likely could have taken their funds with
them.

If all else fails, you need to turn to my friend,
Nicholas Deak. He has the biggest foreign exchange
company in the world, and he states that, for a fee,
he is always able to get assets moved from one country
to another. His address is:

> Nicholas Deak
> Deak-Perera Company
> 29 Broadway
> New York, New York 10006

But let me reemphasize. Taking these measures after
foreign exchange controls are passed by Congress can
cost money and time, and can run the risk of potentially being illegal. If one wants to keep, say, ten
percent of his assets out of the country, the time to
make provision to do that would be now.

SUMMARY AND CONCLUSION

Foreign exchange controls can prevent a citizen from
taking his assets out of a country. We believe it is
wise in this turbulent world, to maintain the largest
number of options. Having ten percent of one's assets
outside of the country in which he lives could prove,
in the long run, to be wise and prudent. It may turn
out to be an unnecessary piece of insurance, as many
fire insurance policies are, but it could also prove
to be very handy in the event of a foreign exchange
fire.

If one is going to move some of his assets out of the
country, it is best to do it now while it is easy and
convenient. But even after controls are instituted,
there are ways to accomplish a capital move, but there
is an extra price to pay in both time and money for
not being prepared.

8

Be prepared for

A GOLD AND SILVER BOOM

Before we examine gold and silver specifically, we need
to first look at some interrelationships. As interest
rates rise, the prices of gold and silver usually rise
too. On the other hand, while interest rates are
rising, the stock market usually declines. Once interest rates top out and start down, then gold and silver usually drop with them, and the stock market begins
its rise.

These basic cycles have occurred consistently in the
past on roughly a four-year interval. You normally see
about two years up in the stock market and two years
down, while in that same four-year period you will see
interest rates and gold and silver falling for the
first two years and rising for the last two years.
Then they simply repeat this cycle.

However, there is an exception to this. In the runaway
inflation in Germany in the 1920's, gold and silver,

the stock market and interest rates all were rising together.

PRICE INCREASE DUE TO INFLATION

You remember back in our earlier chapter we pointed out that at a 25.9 percent average inflation rate, by the year 2000 all prices would be up by a factor of 100. Thus, if gold did nothing but keep up with inflation, it could rise to substantial heights. As I write this, in the fall of 1980, gold is around $600 per ounce. If the inflation rate averages 25.9 percent between now and the year 2000, this would put gold, simply because of inflation, at $60,000 an ounce in the year 2000. Similarly silver is at roughly $15 per ounce, and by the year 2000 at that average inflation rate, silver would be at $1,500 per ounce.

These prices seem unthinkable to the average American today. But accept for a moment the possibility of their reality. What we are looking for is an investment that will not just keep up with inflation but will do better than inflation. In my opinion, both gold and silver will out-perform the average inflation rate over the next ten or twenty years.

THE CASE FOR GOLD

Gold is the only true monetary metal. Today it is the only true store of wealth. It is the only thing recognized in a time of emergency.

For example, when South Viet Nam fell, an ounce of gold would get you a boat ride or a plane ride out of South Viet Nam, and nothing else would - no amount of paper currency, not even diamonds or silver, but only gold. We see the world moving more and more back toward a gold standard and a recognition of the value of gold in international trade.

The demand for gold is not for industrial use but for

monetary use. Governments are minting gold coins and using gold as a national store of wealth.

Back when gold was $42 an ounce, oil was roughly $2 per barrel, and thus an ounce of gold would buy 20 barrels of oil. Today, with gold at $600 and oil at $30, an ounce of gold will still buy exactly 20 barrels of oil. The ratio between gold and oil has not changed. What has occurred is that our paper money has become worth 20 times less, as measured in either of these two valuable commodities, than the currency was worth a short ten years ago.

We have been encouraging the readers of *MSL* to buy gold for many years. We encouraged them to buy when it was less than $50 an ounce. When it pooped out at the end of 1974 at almost $200 per ounce, we then took our people out of gold and recommended they short it. It fell to $105. When it moved back up to $115 we recommended purchasing it again. Thus for the long haul, we don't believe one can go wrong by purchasing gold.

We recommend buying either gold coins or gold bullion through a Swiss bank. We definitely do *not* recommend buying gold bullion bars on which you take delivery. These are difficult to sell and must be reassayed.

THE CASE FOR SILVER

We recommend silver even more highly than we recommend gold. Silver is not only a precious metal, but it is also a highly significant industrial metal. It is used for electrical contacts in computers, in washing machines, in the photographic industry, and in jewelry. It is even used in the military. For example, the batteries in a torpedo require 5,000 ounces of silver, and they are expendable.

The world is using more silver each year than it is producing. This short fall of production over consumption is beginning to catch up with silver, and thus we could see silver easily over $100 per ounce by the end of the 1980's.

As with gold, we recommend buying bags of silver coins. These have a face value of $1,000 but are presently selling for about $12,000 (the fall of 1980). If possible, a family should have a bag of silver coins for each member. If not possible, then they should move to as near this as possible. If a family had to choose to buy either gold coins or silver coins, I would encourage them to move toward the silver coins.

The only way I would encourage anyone to buy silver bullion would be through a Swiss bank. They buy it for you, and store it for you. They also guarantee it is good deliverable silver so that when they sell it, it does not have to be reassayed. You can simply write or wire your Swiss bank telling them to take money out of your current account and buy silver bullion (or gold bullion), and they will complete the transaction for you.

WHAT ABOUT THE SHORT-TERM TRENDS OF SILVER AND GOLD?

To attempt to put short-term trends of silver and gold in a book is difficult since it would probably be obsolete by the time it was printed.

This is why we produce a newsletter, *The McKeever Strategy Letter (MSL)*, to keep our subscribers currently abreast of developments in the gold and silver markets and to advise them on specific points at which to buy and to sell. For further information about *The McKeever Strategy Letter (MSL)*, write to:

> MSL
> P.O. Box 4130
> Medford, Oregon 97501

SUMMARY AND CONCLUSION

I believe that in the long run gold and silver are going to not only keep up with inflation but keep ahead of it. We foresee incredibly high prices for these two precious metals across the coming years for the long-term investor.

We recommend that families have their savings in gold and silver coins. If you wish to save $120 per month, we encourage you to buy a roll of silver quarters each month rather than put it into a savings account. In the long run, we feel this will be much more beneficial. These silver quarters are easily saleable at your local coin store.

For the short-term movements in these precious metals, and for specific times to buy and sell, we recommend the newsletter, *MSL*, to keep you abreast of the current happenings in the precious metals markets.

9

Be Prepared for

A STOCK MARKET BOOM

As we pointed out in our chapter on gold and silver, normally the stock market goes in the opposite direction of the gold and silver market. Then you might ask: how can both the stock market and gold and silver have enormous booms on the horizon? The answer to that is not quite as simple as it looks, but it's also not that complicated.

The stock market and the gold and silver markets could continue to move in opposite directions, but ever upward. Nothing ever goes up in a straight line, and you would still see this same kind of cycle, but with each new cycle being higher than the previous one. Also, when the public truly perceives that hyperinflation has hit the United States, they will be moving rapidly out of cash into gold, silver, the stock market, and anything else they perceive has value. Just as in the runaway inflation in Germany in the 1920's, we could

also see here in America both gold and the stock market
moving up together.

THE BASIC FOUR-YEAR CYCLE

As we mentioned in the chapter on gold and silver,
there is a basic four-year cycle in the stock market.
I believe this is due to the presidential election
occurring every four years. It is likely that if we
had a presidential election every six years, there
would be a six-year cycle in the stock market. Presidents have enormous power to help make the economy
look good before an election. Thus, actions they take
will make roughly the years before and after the election booming ones in the stock market.

At the end of April 1980 I gave a buy signal for the
stock market, recommending that people buy calls and
warrants as well as stocks. The stock market then
moved up dramatically and, according to the Dow theory,
gave a major bull signal when it exceeded 928.67 on
July 21, 1980 with the transports rising to a new high
of 313.43.

Our best projection is that a major bull market started
in April 1980 that will probably last through 1981,
possibly ending in early 1982.

Let me hasten to add that this type of projection is
a very dangerous one to put into a book. By the time
you are reading this, we may well have changed our
minds on this. This again is why we publish a newsletter, *The McKeever Strategy Letter (MSL)*, to keep
our subscribers continually up to date on our recommendations on the stock market. The address to inquire about the newsletter *MSL* is found in the previous
chapter.

ONE MUST TAKE BOLD ACTIONS

When a major move in a commodity or the stock market

takes place, one must be willing to move boldly into that market. Our recommendation then is that you have close trailing stop loss orders that will let the market itself take you out of the market. This way, the average investor does not have to make the decision to sell. The market makes that for him. These close trailing stop loss orders should be placed right below the uptrend line and moved up each week. Once a stop loss order has been moved up it should never be lowered. Thus when the market comes down and breaks through that uptrend line, the individual will be taken out of the stock that he is in.

SUMMARY AND CONCLUSION

We believe that we have seen the beginning of a new stock market which will take the market to new all-time highs. We could be wrong, and we will keep you posted in *MSL*. Inflation, if nothing else, is going to take the stock market up. But added to this, some major four-year cycles and the presidential election should make for a good stock market for about two years. Then, beginning in 1982, we should see the beginning of a decline. However, in the interim get ready, because a stock market boom is coming.

10

Be Prepared for
EMERGENCIES

Reprinted from MISL #197, November 1979

When I was a Boy Scout our motto was *"Be Prepared"*. The leaders tried to help us to "be prepared" for many types of emergencies. They taught us first aid, so that we could be prepared for situations wherein somebody was injured. They gave us wildersness training, so that we could start a fire without matches, build a lean-to out of pine boughs and be able to find food and survive if lost in the woods. I am very grateful for this and all of the other training that I received as a Boy Scout, when I was a young man.

I hope to do a series of articles entitled:

        Be Prepared --- For Wage and Price Controls
        Be Prepared --- For a Banking Crisis
        Be Prepared --- For a Stock Market Boom

As I travel around and talk to people, I find that there are some areas of life in which people are well prepared - perhaps even overprepared - and other areas in which they are not prepared at all. For example, some people are prepared for the eventuality of a fire in their home. They have fire insurance, fire extinguishers and so

forth. On the other hand, in their car they may not have
an adequate set of tools, emergency flares or even a
jack. They intend to rely completely on AAA, forgetting
that one's car can break down out in the middle of a
lonely highway, miles from even a telephone.

One thing that an individual who finds himself in this
position can do is to take a moment to write down the
various emergencies that can occur. With some 3 x 5
cards, one could write one such emergency on the top of
each card and on the rest of that card, put things that
would be desirable preparations to meet that emergency.
One could then sequence these cards, with the emergency
with the highest probability of occurrence on the top,
and the one with the lowest probability of occurrence on
the bottom. Then one could simply start down through the
stack and, in a logical, intelligent way, make preparations to meet those various emergencies.

The preparation I'd like to discuss in this article is
preparation for some type of disaster involving your
home. Some of our subscribers live in Mobile, Alabama,
and, as you know, a little over a month ago it was hit
by Hurricane Frederick. The next section is a letter
from a lady who lives in Mobile, who experienced the
fury and disaster of Hurricane Frederick.

A LETTER FROM MOBILE, ALABAMA

Dear Jim,

This is a post script to Frederick's aftermath in
Mobile from one of your subscribers.

Needless to say this was a brand new experience for
most people. Nevertheless on the whole the quick response of the Civil Defense, National Guard, law en-
forcement personnel, elected officials, Board of
Health, news media and personnel of the power and phone
companies was outstanding. There were some mistakes,
goofs such as conflicting information at times, some
political bickering and a problem in opening public
schools, that kept the schools closed for two weeks.

At no time has the Scripture "joy cometh in the morning" been more meaningful. After the fury of the storm passed my family walked outside and dug our way through a forest of broken limbs, shrubbery and uprooted trees to a beautiful sunrise but unbelievable devastation. During the night the "blackness" could only be compared to being deep within a cave as the guide turns off the lights. The roar of the wind was so loud throughout the night that we did not hear the trees cracking or uprooting around us or parts of neighborhood buildings being blown away. Our world had shrunk overnight to our home and immediate neighborhood and one radio station.

Living on the hill as we do that first morning we were without power, phone or water. There was no electricity to pump the municipal water up to the higher elevations. There was also hardly any transportation, our cars, hauling trailer and motorcycle were under the garage that was under a huge oak which would take 21 days to get removed and be able to pull out the repairable car. We did get the motor out the second day - with a dead battery.

Between our home and 250' down the street to my Mother's were four impassable areas, even to walking. The devastation to vegetation was shocking. By 7:00 A.M. the air was filled (with) the buzz of chain saws and the task of cleaning up had begun. Later that day our pastor was a welcome sight when he passed by on his way to purchase temporary roofing materials. During the days following our church assumed the function of a clearing house for information to relatives calling from over the country inquiring of their families' welfare.

That first day, we used the bicycle to the nearest operating phone some 4 blocks away. A neighbor volunteered a truck, sharing their wheels with us. We ran the truck off siphoned gas from the cars. Gasoline was probably the second hardest thing to come by. Without electricity the pumps won't operate until generators or hand pumps are installed.

Our personal experience was that we were able to rent a car in 2 days, received running water in 3 days, and were in the lucky 25 percent to have power restored

within 4 days. In clean up we found the snakes were
more numerous and biting and stinging insects at times
almost became a plague. The aloe plant was most useful
in relieving pain and itching from yellow jackets
speedily.

My husband, Gene, took a week vacation and almost
single handedly undertook the job of cleaning the yard.
You had to do for yourself as every one was having the
same problems.

The Ice Company where I am employed operated by generator brought in by the guard. With rifle bearing guards
and police constantly present to prevent any possible
riots. (Some of those people were understandably quite
rough.) The Civil Defense dispensed free ice throughout the county for over a week until the power was over
50% restored.

Three weeks have now passed and some phones and power
are still out and many, many streets are stacked high
with highly inflamable vegetative debris. The Corps of
Engineers have undertook the responsibility of letting
out contracts to clear streets and private property for
the city, as an aide to existing crews. There are over
3 million cubic feet to be removed. This is one of the
biggest helps to those of us that suffered minor damage
- minor in comparison to those that lost all their
material possessions.

This storm presented an opportunity for us all to learn
and grow spiritually and obtain first hand experience
in physical survival. I became aware of inner weaknesses and strengths within while trying to cope with a
multitude of unfamiliar problems. Reflecting back on
the past few weeks there is great joy as always in seeing one's prayers answered as they were, in seeing God
meet any and every personal need. (I hope one of the
lessons I learned from Freddie is to pray a more complete prayer. I had neglected to pray for the garage,
vehicles or barn and these were what received the damage at our place.) I thank God for the beautiful peace
he gives his children and pray for those who say they
were so frightened at this time.

Also, I must tell you that the urging for preparation

of emergencies both in MISL and END were quite helpful. I am sure we were more comfortable for the few
preparations we had completed. We had a 55 gal. drum
of kerosene with a hand pump, (this is my greenhouse
heating method), that we were able to share with our
neighbors, a supply of lamps, a S.I. water purifier if
needed, and also the S.I. survivor saw which I found
convenient to use, especially since my husband doesn't
allow me to use his chain saw. The Lord provided the
chain saw last January. Our cooking was done at
Mother's on her propane stove. Frederick won't ever be
forgotten by those of us who experienced it.

If you read through this letter, Jim, what I am really
trying to say is a big thank you and tell you to keep
on keeping on preparing us for whatever the future has
in store.

Yours in Christ,

Mrs. J. H. C.
Mobile, Alabama

COMMENTS ON THE LETTER

In the next to last paragraph, where this subscriber is
talking about an S.I. police flashlight, an S.I. water
purifier, and an S.I. survivor saw, she's referring to
Survival Inc. (S.I.), which is a mail order supply organ-
ization providing all types of survival and self-suffi-
cency items and equipment, as well as dehydrated food.
They have everything from lamps that are a combination
electric and kerosene, and wind and gasoline electrical
generators, to a "doctor's black bag" geared for use by
the layman in the home. They have just come out with
their new catalog. I would encourage you to send $1 for
it (the $1 is refundable on your first purchase) and con-
sider carefully which of these items you should buy. You
can write to them at:

        Survival Inc. (800) 421-2179
        Box 4727
        Carson, CA 90746

If you phone, ask for the President, Bill Pier.

We will deal with the shortages of power, water, gasoline,
phone service and vehicles mentioned in this lady's letter, later in this issue, but first I think that it is
important to note her emphasis on the spiritual side of
life. I would hate to go through something like that
without God. He gave this lady not only peace and joy
through some of this turmoil, but I believe also some
real protection in answer to her prayers. I would like
to encourage all of our readers to seek God and come into a right relationship with Him so that you have His
power available to you during these times of emergencies.
I stand ready to do what I can to assist any of our
readers in their search for the Lord. Please feel free
to give me a call if I can be of help.

EMERGENCIES CAUSED BY EARTHQUAKES

Before commenting on specific areas of preparation, I
would first like to discuss earthquakes. I experienced
the earthquake in Los Angeles in 1971 and was in Guatamala in 1976 between the earthquakes. There was a big
earthquake on Wednesday and one on Friday, and I was
there Thursday. The biggest need at that point in time
was for water, and they were flying it in, in tanker
airplanes. Many of the buildings, including hotels,
were damaged to such an extent that they wouldn't allow
anyone inside them, and there was hardly a window left
unbroken in the entire town. In talking to Paul
Stixrud and his wife, friends of ours who live in
Guatamala and experienced the earthquake firsthand, they
said the noise was deafening, like they were in the middle of a battlefield. All of the bookcases, china cabinets, and liquor cabinets came crashing over; dishes were
flying out of people's cupboards, and hot water heaters
falling over. The amount of noise that was generated was
truly incredible. They said that they would have been
much better off had all of the tall heavy objects in
their home somehow been secured to the wall, so they
could not have toppled.

PREPARATION FOR NATURAL DISASTERS

The disaster from the hurricane and the earthquake had
many things in common. These are the same types of

things that would result from a tornado, a flood, a severe ice and snow storm, sabotage of a power station or
simply power blackout, and so forth. Before examining
preparations that you might want to make, I first would
like to share something.

Some of our long-term readers are likely saying, "Jim,
I've heard much of this before; why are you saying it
again?" The reason is that many of our long-term,
faithful readers, as well as many of our new readers,
have not yet taken the steps necessary to "be prepared"
even for a minor emergency, much less one of major proportions. I felt that including the lady's letter from
Mobile might help motivate people to action. She had
made preparations and was really glad of it. There is
no way that you can predict some types of disasters in
your area. When one strikes, it is too late to begin to
make preparations for it. Because of love and concern
for you, and a desire that you be prepared for an emergency, I am reviewing some of the critical areas.

WATER --- WATER --- WATER

After any emergency that I have seen, the three most important things to have are water, water and water. We
recommend having at least 55 gallons stored for each member of your family. The bare subsistence survival amount
is one gallon per day per person, but to have any for
washing faces, brushing teeth, washing dishes and so
forth it takes much more than that. (55-gallon plastic
water storage barrels are available from Survival Inc.)

It is also handy to have a water purifier in case you
need to drink from your neighbor's swimming pool or a
nearby lake or pond.

One of the reasons that water is so critical is that in
almost every community, even those people with wells rely
on electrical power to pump the water. Thus, when the
power goes (and it will in every one of these emergencies), your water goes with it. You can live forty days
without food, but you can barely live four days without
water.

FIRST AID

There are almost always injuries that accompany thes
types of disasters. Therefore, it is important for t
adults in the family to have good first aid training.
This may take a little time, but it is worth contactir
your local Red Cross, not only for their basic course,
but also for their advanced course.

You are going to need good first aid supplies. Again
Survival Inc. has very good first aid kits of all types
In addition to these kits, you can make triangular ban-
dages out of old sheets, splints out of scrap wood and s
forth, in order to have available supplies for helping
others, in addition to your own family, during times of
emergency. Also you may like to have the layman's "doctor's black bag" in situations like these. You need to
have all of these supplies in your home, located where
everyone knows where they are. Like in Mobile, it may be
a while before you can get to a drugstore to purchase
them, and then you may be too late - their supply may be
gone.

HEAT AND COOKING

The next two or three areas of preparation can most easil
be met with a good camper, mini-motor home or motor home,
if one can afford one of these. With this you could have
a warm place to sleep and cook, and if it had an electrical generator, even run some of the basic power tools fro
it. However, we are going to assume that one does not
have such a vehicle (or a self-contained travel trailer).

Most homes are either heated with gas or electricity. Ir
some disasters, such as earthquake, gas lines will be
broken and gas will not be available. Therefore, an alternate source for space heating and heat for cooking
needs to be available. This can be something as simple
a fireplace. However, fireplaces are terribly inefficie
and we would recommend having a wood stove that fits int
the fireplace. Another advantage is that that wood stov
can also be used for cooking. If a home does not have a
fireplace, a regular wood stove I believe to be the most
desirable alternate source of heat.

It may be that you do not want to have a wood stove si
ting around in one of your rooms. You could have one

stored in the garage, and the flue and pipe already installed, which would carry the smoke outdoors, covered by one of the round covers that would be flush with your wall. Then everything would be ready so that in an emergency you could simply bring in the stove, a couple of lengths of pipe, hook it up and you would be in business. If you do this, don't forget to have a good supply of firewood laid in and dry. (I in no way mean to insult your intelligence, but there have been situations wherein a person had an emergency wood stove and no firewood.)

Another alternative is the camp cookstove and camp heaters that run off of the little bottles of propane. One word of caution about using any of the things mentioned above is that if there is any danger of a gas leak from broken gas lines, be careful about using any kind of a flame (including candles), because of the danger of explosion.

NO LIGHTS, NO CAMERA, NO ACTION

Earthquakes tend to occur about 5 a.m. - 6 a.m. and many other disasters occur at night. If your home were to experience an earthquake tonight, and there were portions of the ceiling fallen down, broken glass, some walls caved in and it was pitch black (because all the lights in the city would be off) what would you do? If it was so black that you couldn't even see your hand in front of your face, how would you go into the other room to check on your children, to see if they were alright or if they needed help, without cutting your feet on glass, stepping on nails, stumbling into fallen lumber?

Most families do not have such a simple thing as a flashlight in the bed stand. An even better thing is available from Survival Inc. It is a little emergency light you plug into a wall socket, which is slightly larger than the regular little night lights. It stays trickle charged by the electrical power. Once the power goes off, these lights come on automatically and last for almost an hour. We have a number of them in our home, because out here on the ranch the power goes off frequently during the winter, from trees falling across power lines. These lights have proven very very valuable to us. In our situation it gives us ample time to light candles and make other provisions.

There is also a fluorescent lamp type of lantern that is
run off of batteries. These would be good for giving
sustaining light for cooking and other purposes during an
extended time of power outage. A good supply of candles
is also desireable. Survival Inc. has an emergency candle that comes packed in a can that lasts for over 50
hours. This type of candle, not the typical tapered
table candle, would be recommended for use during this
kind of emergency.

ELECTRICITY IF AT ALL POSSIBLE

If at all possible, some amount of electricity is extremely desirable. For example, in Mobile and other
similarly hit areas, refrigeration was a real problem.
There were almost riots from people trying to get ice to
preserve food. Most people could not possibly eat all
the food out of their freezer before it spoiled, and
possibly not even all out of their refrigerator, if their
freezer and refrigerator were not operating. Thus, even
enough electricity to run your refrigerator and freezer,
and possibly a light or two, could be very valuable.

If you want to have a little bit of electricity, for the
vast majority of homes this means a gasoline-powered
electrical generator. There are ones available from
Survival Inc., Sears, and many other places. Probably
1500 watts could get the average family by, and about
4500 watts would be about the maximum that most homes
would need.

As far as actually utilizing this generator, one could do
it with a series of heavy-duty, outdoor-type extension
cords, or if one were building a home one could have a
separate series of sockets installed at appropriate
places with an outside receptacle where the generator
could be plugged in. In that case, all that would be
necessary would be to unplug the refrigerator, freezer,
so forth from their normal sockets and plug them into
these when the generator was being used.

However, a generator without any gasoline doesn't do one
any good. There are many books and pamphlets written on
the safe storage of gasoline. We mentioned in MISL a few
issues ago about an Explosafe gasoline can. Gasoline

stored long without any additive will turn to varnish
and become unusuable. Survival Inc. has a chemical
called "Gas Saver" which when added to gasoline will allow it to be stored up to ten years. We continue to recommend that a person have some gasoline stored at home,
if at all possible, provided that it is stored safely.
(You might even want to have your fire department come
out and be sure that you are storing it safely.) As the
gasoline shortage eases up, this storage might become
feasible again.

Another alternative which eliminates the safety storage
problem is to have your gasoline generator converted so
that it can also run off of bottled propane, as well as
gasoline (we've also recommended that you have this conversion made for your car, so that by simply turning a
switch it can run off of either gasoline or propane.)
You could then have one of the large 500-gallon propane
tanks installed in your backyard, run your generator
directly off of that and fill bottles to run your car
from it. We've said all along that natural gas is going
to be much more available in years to come than gasoline,
so this type of conversion could also make some long-
range sense when we get into some real energy shortages
again.

WHAT ABOUT FOOD?

We continue to recommend that you have approximately
three months supply of the food that you normally eat,
stored in your home. However, if this is in frozen form,
you must be able to provide your own electricity to be
sure that it remains frozen during an emergency. There
is an addage in food storage that says *"store what you
eat and eat what you store"*. People who have laid in
large supplies of dehydrated food and never eat it are
going to be in for a bad jolt if they ever switch and
start having to live off of that food. If you are going
to store dehydrated food, you should eat some of it as
you go along; plan to eat about 20% of the food that you
have stored each year, or at least 1% of it per month.
Thus, if you had 200 cans of dehydrated food stored, you
should average eating two to three cans per month. If
you do not do this, I would recommend that you store food
that you do eat, and eat it on a rotating basis.

For most of the emergencies that we have talked about
this article, your three months supply of your regular
food would be very adequate. We still do recommend hav
ing at least a year's supply of food stored for your fa
ily in case of longer-term emergencies and disruptions (
the supply system. However, if one is not prepared in
other ways for the emergencies that we have discussed
thus far, having a year's supply of food is fairly mean-
ingless. We believe you should take first things first
and to be prepared for the kind of emergencies that *have*
happened last year, this year, and are likely to happen,
maybe even in your community, next year.

TAKE ACTION

The key to this is to take action, and actually make som
of these preparations while it is still fresh in your
mind. Perhaps the following list will help act as a
check list for you:

	Target Date	Date Complete
[ ] water stored	_____	_____
[ ] water filter	_____	_____
[ ] first aid kit	_____	_____
[ ] first aid supplies	_____	_____
[ ] "doctor's black bag"	_____	_____
[ ] first aid basic training	_____	_____
[ ] first aid advanced training	_____	_____
[ ] CPR training	_____	_____
[ ] emergency lighting	_____	_____
[ ] emergency heat	_____	_____
[ ] electrical generator	_____	_____
[ ] bicycle	_____	_____
[ ] chain saw	_____	_____
[ ] tall furniture secured to wall	_____	_____
[ ] preparations complete - relax and enjoy life	_____	_____

SUMMARY AND CONCLUSIONS

Major disastors hit cities and towns of the United States every year. These may be hurricanes, tornadoes, floods, earthquakes, or prolonged blizzards. In the future we could have disasters occur because of trucking and train strikes, strikes by firemen, electrical workers, water system employees and by acts of sabotage and terrorism. Because many of these occur suddenly, with no warning, and frequently at night, any preparations that we are going to make need to be made well ahead of time.

11

Be Prepared for

VIOLENCE

Reprinted from MISL #208, June 1980

We here at MISL are concerned about your total
well-being. We are concerned not just about your
financial prosperity, but also about your physical
and spiritual well-being, as well as your liberty
and freedom. What good does it do you to prosper
financially if physically or spiritually you are
in a dangerous position, or if you lose your
liberty?

For those of you who have subscribed to MISL primarily for financial insights, we trust that you
will be patient as we occasionally venture over
into one of these other areas; perhaps you will
even benefit from these discussions. We all need
to be aware of what is happening in our world, and
we must try to foresee what is coming and prepare
for it as best we can. Back in MISL #197 we said
we were going to have a series of articles on
being prepared. We have already covered:

        Be Prepared for . . . Emergencies
        Be Prepared for . . . Wage and Price Controls

In forthcoming issues we will deal with such subjects as:

    Be Prepared for . . . Foreign Exchange
        Controls
    Be Prepared for . . . A Banking Crisis
    Be Prepared for . . . Runaway Inflation

People hear enough about what is happening in the
world; we find that what they want are some practical suggestions as to what they can do to be
ready for the things that are coming.

In this particular issue we would like to talk
about being prepared for . . . VIOLENCE. Of
everything that we could potentially experience,
violence is one that could strike any of us at
any time, and yet it is the one thing that most
people are least prepared to handle. Violence
could occur from natural sources such as volcanoes, tornadoes, hurricanes, earthquakes, or tidal
waves; or it could come from man-made sources
such as war, terrorism, kidnapping, rape, robbery
or mugging. You might think, "But none of these
things would ever happen to me," and that is
exactly what every victim of any of these acts of
violence thinks beforehand. It is this mental
attitude that causes us to be totally unprepared
to react properly and swiftly to the crises of
violence.

VIOLENCE FROM NATURE

Most violent events in nature give us some warning ahead of time. We may see hurricanes forming in the Caribbean, or the conditions may be
right for tornadoes. Small earthquakes or
ground swellings may signal potential volcanic
action, and floods are usually preceded by flood
warnings. The only possible exception to this
is an earthquake itself. However, even earth-

quakes are beginning to give us clues that we can take as early warnings. The earthquake in China a few years ago was well-predicted, and thus the loss of life was minimized by evacuating some of the major cities.

If violence in nature gives us some warning, why are so many people caught unprepared, losing their homes, property, and even their lives? I believe the reason is that people, in general, are not aware of danger and tend to foolishly ignore warnings, believing, like the ostrich, that danger will not strike them if they put their heads into the sand and ignore it. I am not saying that we should live in fear, but to ignore potential danger is indeed very foolish.

For example, tornadoes are caused by a unique combination of weather and atmospheric phenomena. The stage is set when we have a cold air mass riding up above a warm air mass. The cold air wants to sink to the ground, and the warm air mass is in the way. When the cold air is able to punch down through the warm air, it does so with violence, sometimes in the form of a tornado. When these conditions exist, the weather bureau puts out a tornado warning to the areas of potential danger. Having lived a number of years in Texas (which is part of the tornado alley that includes most of the Midwest), once or twice a year we had such a tornado warning. When there was a tornado warning, what did the average person do that was different from his regular life routine? The answer is *nothing,* absolutely nothing. He went about his everyday life as if there were no tornado warning at all. I did the same thing back in those days although I would not now because I have become more conscious of danger and violence.

In the earlier days in Texas (and in the rest of the tornado alley) people built storm cellars which were also used for root cellars, where they stored the root vegetables such as potatoes, carrots, and so forth. When conditions looked as if a tornado might be coming, the family went into the root cellar and spent a day, or even more, until the danger was past. They may have experienced damage of property, but they would not have experienced loss of life. Some farmers even went to the extent of having a storm cellar for some of their prized livestock. They were aware of the potential danger of tornadoes. When one seemed imminent, they did something to protect the lives of their families, their livestock, and, as much as possible, their property.

What could a family in today's world do to protect itself from tornadoes? They could, like the farmers of a few years ago, build some type of a storm cellar. If it is well-designed, it could function as a cool storage place for food, and it could also double as a nuclear fallout shelter. If a tornado warning were given, the children could remain home from school, the father could stay home from work, and they could spend the day in their storm cellar, monitoring the weather situation on their transistor radio. Less drastic, they could just stay home and monitor the weather situation, and then move to the storm cellar if it looked like danger was near. But either way they would be in a location where they had stored food and water and other emergency supplies, and they would be together. (When a tornado struck Dallas, I saw fathers try to dash home to see if their families were alright. It would be terrible not knowing if your family was safe or not.) But, you say, the father would miss a day of work, and the children would miss a day of school. The same thing was certainly true of our forefathers of yesteryear. For some reason we have placed "not missing a day of school" higher on our priority list than protecting our families from the dangers of nature. It

133

is this type of thinking that is endangering the
lives of individuals and families all across
America.

That family indeed might miss one or two days a
year at work and school because of tornado warnings. This might go on for five or ten years.
Yet perhaps the eleventh year would be the year
of the disaster that struck their home. Would
all of the days of missed school and missed work
be worth it? It certainly would be, in my opinion.

We have elaborated a bit on tornadoes because of
the one that recently struck near Kalamazoo,
Michigan, but tornadoes are simply a typical example. You could use a similar approach in looking at hurricanes. Even before the days of
satellites, the airline pilots and ship captains
would give warning of a hurricane forming. However, today with our satellite photographs, we can
actually see them forming in the Caribbean and can
chart their direction and speed. In fact, in many
areas you can almost forecast the hour when a hurricane will strike. Having plenty of warning, a
family could leave the area and its home, or it
could make storm cellar provisions similar to
those in the tornado-prone area. In some hurricane situations, people have given hurricane parties in frame-constructed buildings right on the
beach; everyone drank heavily and ridiculed the
hurricane. Many people have lost their lives at
such hurricane parties. These people may think
they are showing a semblance of bravery, but to me
they are giving strong proof of their stupidity.
There are times when we calculate the danger and
choose to ignore it for some noble cause. For
example, we may rush into a house on fire to save
a child. But to ignore danger because of neglect
or carelessness or macho pride is one of the most
ridiculous acts a human can perform. The intelligent and wise thing to do is to be aware of po-

tential danger and violence, and take appropriate actions.

VIOLENCE FROM EARTHQUAKES

Many areas in the United States are subject to an occasional earthquake. There are some places, however, that are subject to frequent earthquakes. If you live in an earthquake-prone area, it is certainly not wise to totally ignore earthquakes. That may sound almost trite or naive, but thousands of individuals remain apathetic, ignoring formidable earthquake dangers even in Southern California. There are some houses that are built half on one side of the San Andreas fault and half on the other side. It is well-known that the San Andreas fault is the line that divides two geologic tectonic plates. The American plate, on which rests most of the United States, is moving roughly westward, and the Pacific plate is moving roughly northwest. These plates are passing each other at about five centimeters a year. Where these plates can pass freely, as in Central California, this movement is well-documented and measured. However, the plates have been stuck for over 100 years in the Southern California area, and are not moving past each other at all. Once this sticking breaks loose, they will probably regain all of their lost movement at one time. Geologists vary on how big a movement would occur if the plates suddenly made up for their lack of movement in the past. The best estimates are that the movement would be about 10 to 20 yards. All geologists agree that a major earthquake there is inevitable. The only question is *when* it will occur.

Thus, if a person were buying a home in the Southern California region, would it be wise if he inquired about the proximity of the San Andreas fault? Certainly it would be. But most home

buyers are so unaware and unconcerned that they
do not even ask a simple question like that.
Many realtors are of the ilk that they would not
volunteer that information even if they knew it.
There are other well-known fault lines in the
Southern California area, such as the Long Beach
fault, about which one should also inquire. If
a person owns a home in Southern California (or
near the earthquake-prone region) it would
behoove him, it seems to me, to find out where
the fault lines are in relation to his home.
Obviously, the farther from the fault line, the
safer a structure will be.

With this information, an individual could decide
whether or not to buy, or perhaps even whether to
sell his existing home and move. If for some
reason a person feels that he needs to continue
to live in an earthquake-prone region, there are
many things he can do to prepare for earthquakes.
These are outlined in detail in my book, Christians Will Go Through the Tribulation -- and how
to prepare for it, so we won't get into them now.
Suffice it to say that the water lines will be
severed, thus the storage of water is important.
Gas lines and electrical lines will be broken,
thus it will be important to be able to cook
without gas or electricity. Sewage and waste
disposal will be a problem. All of these contin-
gencies need to be considered. Also, anchoring
any tall, heavy objects such as bookcases and hot
water heaters by strapping them with cable to a
wall can avoid the damage that comes when these
inevitably fall over during an earthquake.

What we are encouraging you to do (and we will
keep repeating this throughout the article) is
to raise your level of alertness to danger. You
should be sensitive in these areas when you are
buying a home or considering an area in which to
live. If you live in an area of potential dan-

ger, provisions and plans should be made in the
event that the violence actually occurs while you
are there.

VIOLENCE FROM VOLCANOES AND FLOODS

Mt. St. Helens in southern Washington did not
erupt without giving several weeks of warning.
There were many earthquakes daily as well as minor
eruptions before the major eruption came. Geologists kept warning of the danger of a major eruption and even warned of the danger of flooding
because a major eruption would melt the snow that
existed in huge quantities on top of the volcano.
The warning signs that Mt. St. Helens gave were
typical of the signs that a volcano gives before
it erupts. There is a bulging of the surface of
the volcano, as can be measured by inclinemeters;
there are earthquakes that can be measured with
seismographs; and there are surface and subsurf-
ace temperatures that can be measured. From this
mass of evidence, the internal mechanisms going
on within the volcano can be determined with some
degree of accuracy.

With all this advance warning, authorities tried
to get loggers, caretakers, and hunters to move
out of the danger area. What was their response?
They fought and resisted their evacuation. In
fact some, such as old Harry Truman, simply re-
fused to leave. Communities that were located
on the banks of the rivers below the volcano were
given warnings of potential flood danger. These
communities basically continued as though no
danger existed. We need to ask ourselves the
difficult question, "why?". Why did these people
refuse to leave, going on as though no danger
existed at all?

We cannot answer in every case. Some may have
felt that they were old and had lived a full life

and were willing to die in comfortable, familiar
surroundings if such an event occurred. However,
I suspect that the majority simply felt that the
authorities were being overcautious and overly
reactive, and that no major eruption was going to
occur. Many lost their lives simply because they
ignored the warnings.

What would have happened had they heeded the
warnings? The logging operators and subcontrac-
tors may have lost a few weeks or even a couple
of months of income from the logging operations.
The people in the communities and the caretakers
of lodges may have had to go live with relatives
or even rent places a safe distance from the
volcano and the river. Perhaps it would have
cost them a few hundred dollars in extra rent
or some financial loss from their businesses.
For some individuals, it might even have cost
them a job because of an irate employer. However, it is difficult for me to see that any of
these costs were too high a price to pay for
their lives and the lives of their children.
Yet financial considerations were doubtless a
major factor in many individuals' decisions to
stay. For some, the relocating of their families to a safer, higher location would have
meant only a couple of months' extra rent. Many
could probably have commuted back to their jobs
or businesses with little or no loss of income.
Thus the financial cost would have been really
very low.

Probably one of the basic underlying reasons why
people ignore such warnings is that we have lost
our healthy fear of danger. Our earlier pioneer
forefathers were continually alert to danger from
every side -- danger from angered Indians, bands
of outlaws, cattle rustlers, and hundreds of
other sources. There was danger from wild animals such as mountain lions, bears, wolves, and
rattlesnakes. There was danger from violent

storms, tornadoes, hail, and other acts of nature.
They also had to be continually on the alert for
danger from fire that could be caused by a care-
less match or lantern. There were no fire de-
partments in those days, and if their homes or
belongings caught on fire they, and possibly
their neighbors, had to put it out. These people
were also hunters, and developed a sensitivity to
any unusual sound or movement. By being alert to
danger they were usually able to either avoid it
or be prepared for it.

On the other hand, our mentality today is basically: "Somebody is going to take care of me." We
don't have to worry about starving to death because the government will give us handouts or
food stamps. We don't have to worry about being
without a house because somebody is going to provide a house whether it be the Red Cross, the
Good Will, or some other group. We don't have to
worry about being without a job because unemployment insurance will take care of us or welfare if
that runs out. We don't have to be worried about
fires because there is a fire department. And
our mentality says that we don't have to be worried about burglaries and rape and such things
because we have the police to take care of us.
We have thus mentally subcontracted or given away
to other people the responsibility for our protection from danger.

I suspect that if you could probe into the sub-
conscious minds of those who died as a result of
the Mt. St. Helens eruption and subsequent
floods, you would find that they had little fear
because they felt that either it would not happen
or if it did, someone would take care of them.

I believe that we, as heads of our homes and families, need to regain what our forefathers had
and become continually aware of and alert to the

dangers around us. I believe that we need to
take back the responsibility for the protection
of ourselves and our families from danger, and
place it squarely on our own shoulders. It may
be that these other institutions and entities
will be able to help, but the responsibility
should be ours and ours alone.

I believe that we should say a general word about
floods before we leave this topic. Buying a
house near a major river, particularly one which
is flood prone, is about as foolish as buying a
home which straddles the San Andreas fault. You
know that the crisis is going to occur. It's a
matter of *when*. It is even more foolish for
those whose homes have been destroyed by floods
to go back and rebuild a home on the very same
site. Frequently people simply do nothing when
flood warnings are given. Then the flood hits,
as predicted, and these people crawl up on their
rooftops and are annually rescued by someone in
a rowboat or, in worse cases, by a helicopter.
Again, they are relying on "someone to take care
of them."

Why do they stay in their homes when they know a
flood is coming? I think for the same reasons
that we discussed above. If they are worried
about their homes being broken into or looted,
they could take all of their valuables and
irreplaceable momentoes with them to a motel
for just 24 hours until the danger of the crest
of the flood is past, and then return to their
homes. It may be that some of them might not be
able to afford staying in a motel; they could
always stay with friends or go to high ground
and camp out in a tent. Again, I believe the
basic reason is that they think it will not
happen or perhaps someone will prevent it or if
it does happen they will be taken care of.

In short, with floods, as with any potential disaster, people need to be alert to the danger, take responsibility squarely on their own shoulders for the protection of themselves and their families, and then take appropriate actions.

VIOLENCE FROM TIDAL WAVES

As a result of underwater earthquakes, underwater volcanic eruptions, and even land-based earthquakes, tidal waves of up to 400 feet have been recorded. It is estimated by some geologists that the earth has experienced, in its geologic history, tidal waves of up to 2,000 feet high. Individuals and families living along a seacoast at an elevation of less than 2,000 feet should at least be aware of the potential dangers of tidal waves.

If a major earth upheaval occurs, such as a massive movement along the San Andreas fault in Southern California, we could experience tidal waves of 1,000 feet in height or better. We know that earthquakes of this magnitude have occurred in Southern California before, because geologically we know that the east coast of Catalina Island (which is 29 miles off the coast of Los Angeles) is identical to the west coast of Palos Verdes Peninsula. In geologic past these were either connected and subsequently separated by an incredible, gigantic earthquake, or the twenty-nine-mile-wide section of land between them sank into the ocean. In either case, it would have created a tidal wave of incredible proportions.

The magnitude and speed of tidal waves can be calculated quite precisely, and thus the time of arrival at a particular seacoast town and its magnitude at arrival can be predicted with a great deal of accuracy. Thus, if a tidal wave

warning were given to a town, everyone would
evacuate to higher ground. Right? Wrong!
In Hilo, on the big island of Hawaii, there was
a big tidal wave around 1950 (I've forgotten the
exact date). This was predicted and the people
were warned. Always preceding a tidal wave's
impact on the coast, there is an incredible
drawback of the water to the extent that almost
all of Hilo Bay became dry land. What did the
people do? They went down to the beach to see
this incredible phenomenon of Hilo Bay being dry.
They thought that the predictors were wrong and
that they were having a water recession rather
than a tidal wave. Then, of course, with incredible speed the tidal wave came roaring in and
killed hundreds of people as well as destroying
all of the buildings in the waterfront area.
That tidal wave, in comparison to most, was actually a fairly small one.

Why didn't the people who lived there in Hilo
flee to the mountains? Some of them did, but
most of them ignored the danger, exhibited curiosity, and unfortunately lost their lives in
the process.

I won't reiterate what they should have done, but
you know that they should have been more alert to
the real danger of the impending disaster; they
should have acted responsibly and moved to higher
ground with their families and anything that was
precious to them.

FREEDOM IN DANGER FROM APATHY

Just as people seem to be numb to the real danger
from the various acts of nature, it appears that
most Americans are also numb to the real danger
that lies in the political arena. If we are not
aware of the danger there and alert to it, then,
just like the people experiencing a tornado warn-

ing, we will do nothing and assume that the danger
really does not exist and if it does, those who
are crying out the warning are exaggerating and
are really alarmists and therefore should be
ignored.

In the political arena, we are in danger of losing
almost all, if not indeed all, of our personal
liberties here in America. We no longer really
have personal property. We are renting our homes
and our land from the government, and if you do
not believe this, simply stop paying your property
tax and they will come and sell "your" home or
ranch to pay the property taxes. You cannot do
with your property what you would like. You have
to get the government's approval to dig a well,
build a septic tank, subdivide, build another
house, or start a business in your home. Similarly, we cannot employ who we would like and pay
them what we would like. The government tells us
exactly who we can hire and how much we have to
pay them. The government tells us what working
conditions we have to provide and even how many
coffee breaks a day. The government tells us how
much interest we can charge (or be charged) on
loans. They can raise interest rates and create
a recession if they wish to, can make the owning
of something like gold illegal, and on and on.
If the American people do not do anything, this
trend will continue, and they will have progressively less and less personal freedom until eventually they have basically none at all.

Similarly, on the international scene, the world
is in ever-increasing danger of being entirely
taken over by communism. But most Americans
aren't concerned. They figure, "They'll be
stopped." But when they are faced with the question, "Who will stop them and where?," they have
no answers, but they have a lot of blind faith
that it will happen. If Americans are not alert
to the danger, they are not going to be doing

anything about it.

TO BE CONTINUED

When I began this article, I had hoped to talk
about how to be prepared for violence in nature,
in the political arena, from war, from terrorism,
and from crime. Unfortunately, it was a bigger
subject than I had anticipated, and we will have
to continue it, hopefully in the next issue.

One of the reasons I wanted to deal with terrorism and related subjects is that the CIA and FBI
are learning some interesting things from their
interviews with the Cubans who are arriving as
refugees, many of whom are highly respected engineers and technical people. From the information gained, the CIA has concluded that Castro
either has nuclear devices or is about to have
them. The impact of Cuba having nuclear devices
and the planes and missiles to deliver these
nuclear devices to most major cities in the
United States is extremely significant. If the
Cubans were to hit us with a nuclear strike,
would the United States send nuclear missiles to
Russia in retaliation? On what basis? . . .
Would Castro still like to teach the U.S. a
lesson and take us down a notch or two? I believe he would.

The CIA is also convinced that many of the Cuban
refugees are really Cuban operatives sent here to
eventually create terrorism within the United
States. Their activities could eventually range
from blowing up electrical and water plants to a
nuclear blackmail from suitcase-style nuclear
devices planted in major cities in the United
States.

Kidnapping and hostage taking are becoming more
and more commonplace. Violent crimes and rape

are becoming more widespread in cities. This is
another subject that we had hoped to deal with
in this article.

There are many things that one can do to be alert
to and prepared for danger, whether it be from
nuclear war, terrorism, or violent crime. Most
of these will have to wait until the next issue
for discussion. However, I feel that I should
mention one now. The best thing an individual
could do for himself and his family is to move
to a small town, not on the seacoast, not in tornado alley, not in a high earthquake risk area,
and not in a flood-prone area. By this move, he
would generally be protected from any of the
violent acts of nature.

Also, since most of the violent crimes, acts of
terrorism, and nuclear blackmail will be commit-
ted in the major cities, he and his family could
be spared many of these man-made violences. You
may wish to use your vacation to look for property in a smaller town and actually purchase it,
whether you are going to occupy it immediately
or at some point in the future. Further considerations on moving from a city to a smaller
town will have to wait for the next issue.

In the meantime, raise your level of alertness
and awareness to danger. The danger could come
from nature, the political arena, a war, or other
people. Do not live in fear, but be alert and
aware. And realize that the responsibility for
the protection and safekeeping of yourself and
your family rests solely on your shoulders and
no one else's. Once you have raised your level
of alertness and assumed this responsibility,
then you can begin to make some intelligent plans
and take some intelligent actions to prepare
beforehand for danger and violence.

More on

VIOLENCE

Reprinted from MISL #209, June 1980

This article is a part of our "Be Prepared For
. . ." series, and is really a continuation of
the article from the last issue of MISL. In
the last issue, which was entitled "Be Prepared
For . . . Violence," we dealt with violence from
geologic upheavals, tidal waves, tornadoes and
other natural phenomena. Although these can
strike any of us at any time, most people remain
unconcerned. I believe that weather-wise and
geologic-wise, we are entering an era of progressively heavier violence. If this is true,
we should, of course, place greater emphasis in
our thinking on these acts of natural violence
than we have in past years.

I just returned from Des Moines, Iowa, where I
spoke at "Rejoice '80," a Christian conference.
In the first week of June they had an incredibly
radical weather phenomenon. They had hail the
size of grapefruit. The amount and force of
these falling ice balls, weighing 2-3 pounds,

were so violent that bark was stripped from trees and many crops were ruined. The people who had given no thought to preparation for violence from weather consequently made no provision to protect their animals or even their own families, and many of them suffered severe damage and even death.

In this issue, we would like to switch from considering violent acts of nature, which could damage us personally, to consideration of man-made violence. This could be either as a result of war (probably nuclear) or from an individual attack against you or your family by thieves, muggers, terrorists, kidnappers, or rioters.

THE FOUR CONDITIONS

There are four conditions that a person can find himself in. I have seen these categories used by other writers to mean various things, but I would like to give you my definitions of them.

Condition White: In this condition, you are completely relaxed. There is basically no alertness to any potential danger. It is a very oblivious condition.

Condition Yellow: In this condition, you become alert to any potential danger that you might encounter. There is no tenseness at all, but there is a mental alertness when you are in this condition. If there is a sudden sound or movement, then your alertness causes you to be ready to act.

Condition Orange: You shift from condition yellow to condition orange when there is a danger present that can harm property. This property might be your home, your automobile, your wallet, your purse, or any other of your possessions.

Condition Red: This is the condition you go into when there is a danger present that could harm your person or the bodies of people whom you are concerned about.

Most people, unfortunately, spend most of their time in condition white. They are unaware of any potential dangers that might be around, whether from nature or from man. And even if they vaguely think of those, they tend to, as we discussed last time, assume that someone else will take care of the danger and protect them.

There are other people who are usually in condition yellow, particularly when they are working. One example of this is a pilot. When I took my pilot training, we checked our gauges and dials about every 30 seconds and we continually asked ourselves, "If the engine quit now, where would we set this 'baby' down?" At one point the answer might be, "On that golf course." A few minutes later I would re-ask the question and the answer might be, "On that highway." Later I might answer, "In that farmer's field." Pilots must be continually in condition yellow, alert to any possible dangers, planning the actions they will take if danger materializes.

For example, while I was taking flying instruction, I once dropped one of the charts on the floor of the plane. I bent down to pick it up, and was about halfway down when I raised back up quickly and pulled the nose of the plane up. When the instructor asked me why I did that, I said, "The sound of the motor changed, and I could tell we were beginning to fall." This is being in condition yellow continually, which is a necessity when you are in a situation like flying.

Other professions constantly require their people to be in condition yellow while at work. One

example of this might be a doctor or nurse.
Things can go wrong with patients at any time,
whether it be in a maternity ward, critical ward,
operating room, or even one of the regular wards.
They are constantly on the alert for danger signs
and are trained in what specific actions to take
when those danger signs occur and the danger
appears to be real.

I find it a helpful exercise to periodically
check to see which condition I'm in - white,
yellow, orange, or red. I personally am almost
never in condition white. Even when sitting at
home relaxing and watching television, if there
is an unusual noise around the ranch, I am very
much on the alert to check it out and to take
appropriate action if necessary. I know some
people who are absolutely never in condition
white and always remain in condition yellow.

Some readers might think that this is a mili-
taristic, warlike, red-neck type of attitude to
remain basically in condition yellow. Yet, if
we turn back to the Bible, it is interesting to
see that this was a biblical principle. When
God told Gideon to choose an army, several thou-
sand people appeared. As a test to see who was
really qualified, Gideon asked them all to take
a drink from the river. Most of the people ran
down to the river, stuck their faces into the
water, totally oblivious to any potential danger
(they were in condition white), and they were
rejected. Those who went down to the river,
scooped some water up into their hands, and
drank from their hands while surveying the
horizon, were chosen. These chosen people were
constantly in condition yellow. They were not
worried about danger or petrified of it, but
they wanted to be alert to it in the event it
came their direction.

A practical application of utilizing the yellow

condition would be the typical family camping
trip. At some time or other just about everyone
enjoys a family campout, and unfortunately we
often take our "condition white" mentality along.
Our daily life in the "civilized" world with its
built-in protective environment (however flimsy
in reality) can lull us into a perpetually-
relaxed mental state. Even though we go camping
for relaxation and recreation, we must remember
that when we walk away from "home" and into the
woods or wilderness, we are leaving a complex
set of life-support systems and entering a survival type of situation that is generally under-
estimated.

Many unfortunate hunting and camping accidents
happen because people are in condition white
while out in the woods. For example, if there
is a fallen tree, most people will step over it,
not realizing that snakes love to stretch out
parallel to fallen tree trunks. By stepping over
it they invite a snake bite from a startled
snake. (One should step on top of a fallen
tree and then take a giant step over and away
from it. One will do this if he is in condition
yellow and aware of the potential danger.)
Similarly, in areas where there are regular
flash floods, people (in condition white) have
been known to choose a campsite in a river bed
because it was nice and sandy and there was no
brush to clear. They subsequently drowned as a
flash flood with a wall of water ten feet high
came down and covered them and their camp. Certainly campsites should be chosen while in condition yellow, looking for potential danger from
flash floods, from a campfire setting a tree on
fire, from rocks falling from an overhanging
ledge, and so forth. I think you get the general
idea that, particularly when we are in a strange
environment such as the woods, I believe it is
absolutely essential to stay in condition yellow.

150

Without trying to lay any heavy trips on anyone, my general observation is that most people spend far too much time in condition white, and are not alert to potential danger, either from nature or from man.

SHIFTING TO CONDITION ORANGE OR RED

Nature does some of the shifting for us. When a real danger to our property or person is present, our adrenalin starts flowing, and it gets us up for either "flight or fight." This usually is an automatic, biological function given to us by God, over which we have no control. However, the average person, when this happens, has not thought through any predetermined plans of action. Even with adrenalin pumping, he tends to stand there, petrified while he is trying to make a decision as to whether he should fight or run. In making the decision to fight, he is also trying to decide what to fight with, whether or not he is really willing to hurt his attacker, and so forth. Hundreds of decisions run through his mind, basically immobilizing him and making him subject to harm.

An airplane pilot is continually saying, "If my engines quit, where will I set this plane down?," or the nurse is saying, "If the heart stops I will immediately go to CPR or an electrical stimulator." A wise automobile driver has thought through in advance what he will do if his brakes fail. For example, he might plan to first turn off the ignition to see if the engine will stop the car; and if that does not work, he is willing to sacrifice the transmission for protection of his person and property by shifting either into low or reverse. Some drivers occasionally pretend their brakes have gone out and take the appropriate action just to see how their cars will respond and how long it takes to stop so that

when they have a real emergency they will know
which action is the most appropriate.

We can say, then, that the preferable and intelligent way to shift from condition yellow into
either condition orange or red, is to have "pre-
thought" as much as possible the specific actions
that you will take when a particular danger presents itself.

ARE YOU WILLING TO HARM ANY ATTACKER?

You notice the question was not, "Do you *want* to
harm any attacker?". I think only sadistic
individuals want to harm people. The real question is: Are you *willing* to harm someone if your
person is attacked or your property is attacked?
I do not have the answer to that for everyone.
I know of people who come at it from completely
opposite directions.

There are those who say, "I in no way want to
get physically involved in protecting property."
If a robber comes into a store, the owner says ,
"Take all the money in the cash register; it's
insured, and I'm not going to try to stop you."
Others with the same conclusions about property
say that if they discover a robber in their
house, they will let him take what he wants
rather than risk any physical harm coming to
them. Similarly, some women have concluded that
if their purse is snatched, they will not try
to hold on to the purse while the purse snatcher
is tugging at the other side. They prefer not
to risk being harmed over a purse.

Others have taken the opposite point of view and
feel that their property is a very private,
important thing to them, and they are willing to
even shoot or kill a robber who is trying to take
their personal possessions. Here at MISL head-

quarters, we receive a lot of unusual things in
the mail. Recently we received a decal that
people can put on their doors and windows that
contains the following message:

> THE OWNER OF THIS PROPERTY IS ARMED
> AND IS WILLING AND ABLE TO PROTECT
> IT. THERE IS NOTHING IN HERE WORTH
> DYING FOR.

As you can see, people of this mentality, who
post such notices, are ready to defend their
property to the nth degree.

On the other hand, one must consider that there
is property and then there is property. If someone is going to take a television set, that is
one thing. But if there is a nationwide famine
or food shortage, because of truckers and rail-
road strikes, and someone comes in to steal your
last two months of food, then taking your food
may be very analogous to trying to harm your
body. Potentially, if he took all of your food
and you were left without any, you and your
family could indeed starve to death.

This takes us to the question of what if there
is a mugger or a kidnapper or a terrorist that
appears with the obvious intent of harming you
physically or even killing you. Or what if someone appears with a knife or a gun and is coming
in your direction, or is moving toward a member
of your family or someone close to you. Most
people are willing, if they stop and think about
it, to risk some bodily harm in order to protect
themselves or their loved ones from actual physical harm.

I am not for or against the use of defensive
violence to meet danger. What I do feel is that
a person should carefully think through what he

is willing or not willing to do once he shifts
from condition yellow to orange or red. It may
be that he wishes to do some things for which
he does not have the skill (karate or shooting).
By predetermining what he wants to do, he can
take appropriate training if necessary.

MILD METHODS OF DEFENSE

The very mildest form of defense is to flee.
In the face of danger there is nothing cowardly
about running and attempting to avoid physical
confrontation. If a woman is on a street and
is being accosted, she should not walk fast but
literally run to a store, policeman, or anything
else. Once I was on a subway in New York; it
was late at night, and a suspicious character
got on the car with me. He may have been per-
fectly innocent, but I didn't like his looks,
so I simply got up and moved to a different car.

Unfortunately, in many instances it seems we have
become a nation of sheep, and will not even run
when danger presents itself. There was the case
of a lady who stopped at a red light. A burly
character opened her car door and got in, subsequently doing her some physical harm including
rape. When asked why she didn't press hard on
the accelerator the moment he opened the car
door, her response was, "The light was still
red." Even though there were no cars coming in
either direction, she sat there and allowed the
man to come into the car because she did not want
to run a red light. We must remember that in
times of danger the rules all change, and probably
it would be a good idea to run a red light and,
in some situations, even hit another vehicle
to avoid some types of danger. Unfortunately,
when the woman got into her car she was in condition white. If she had been in condition
yellow, she would have at least locked the doors.
So we see one can flee even when in an automobile.

The price of a ticket for running a red light,
I am sure the lady would agree, would have been
well worth it.

Similar cases have been recorded where some
youths have flagged down a car. In one case, a
boy stood in front of the car while the others
broke a window and climbed inside. The man would
not move the car forward because he "did not want
to harm the youth." The end result was that he
was beaten almost to the point of death in thanks
for his not wanting to harm anyone. You need to
think through beforehand how much harm you are
willing to do to a person who attacks you.

Another very mild but effective method of defense
is spray paint. You will find that many of the
lacquers you can buy in hardware stores or hobby
shops have warnings on them: Do not get in your
eyes. This warning is valid, because it burns
like blue blazes if you do. A woman could keep
a small can of yellow spray paint of this eye-
irritating type in her automobile at all times.
If an attacker did come up to her at night, she
could roll down the window one inch and spray
him right in the face with the yellow paint.
The burning of the eyes will render him harmless
for at least 30 minutes. It is also easy for
the police to track down somebody with a big
patch of yellow paint in the middle of his face.

Another thing you could do would be to have a
C.B. radio in your car. I realize that the C.B.
craze has passed, but a lady on a lonely road
with a flat tire may find that a C.B. radio
frequently brings help. It does have some
drawbacks, but it is probably much safer than
if she tried to get out and change the tire
herself or walk along a dark road to a service
station. Many C.B.ers would have heard the cry
for help, and it is unlikely that one bad one

would try to take advantage of the situation
because he would know that possibly others were
on their way.

MEDIUM METHODS OF SELF DEFENSE

If one decides that passive methods, such as
running, yellow paint, or a C.B. radio, are
insufficient preparations, and if one is willing
to do a mild amount of bodily harm to an attacker, there are other things that can be very helpful. For example, many things that people frequently have with them are very excellent weapons.
The corner of a book can be a very potent weapon
when jabbed into someone's solar plexus or face.
A rattail comb or a key can be used as a similar
weapon. Fingernails gouging into a person's
face and eyes are very powerful weapons. In
addition, every person carries with him ten very
able weapons. They are: two hands, two elbows,
two feet, two knees, one head, and one mouth.
It is unlikely that an attacker can immobilize
all ten of your weapons at once. You will have
at least one of them with which to fight back
and defend yourself from the attacker.

Your most potent weapons are your hands. When
an attacker grabs you by the arm or the throat
or around the chest or wherever, if you simply
grasp his little finger and pull back until it
breaks, he will be immobilized from the pain.
Unfortunately, many people are so conditioned
that they will allow severe harm to come to their
person rather than break an attacker's finger.
Similarly, a hard step down on a person's foot
can break his arch and render an attacker immo-
bile. You will usually have your feet free, and
this is something that can be done in almost
every situation. We will not get into all of
the other things that one can do, but just be
aware that you have a lot of very potent weapons,

and your attacker has many very vulnerable places
on his body. But, what you are willing to do
should be pre-decided.

STRONG METHODS OF SELF-DEFENSE

Most of the strong methods in self-defense
require some type of training. These would
include one of the martial arts, such as karate,
or the use of weapons. There was a case of a
young lawyer leaving his law firm in New York
City late at night. Three muggers attacked him.
This lawyer happened to have been well along in
karate training. He flattened all three of them
and stood over them daring one of them to get up
while he called for the police. (Very shortly
after that, all of the lawyers in his firm decided they would start studying karate.) Karate
does not depend on one's size. There is a 100
pound lady who is teaching karate to the marines,
and she has no challengers among her six-foot-
plus students. The martial arts can be utilized
as a good physical conditioning exercise as well
as providing some means of self-defense. One
does not have to get into martial arts philosophy or become a "militant" in order to learn
simple self-defense. Many of the YMCA's and
YWCA's have very good self-defense programs for
both men and women.

In some ways, an even stronger method of self-
defense, when one goes into condition orange or
red, is the use of weapons. There are a number
of types of weapons, such as crossbows and blow
guns, but when most people think of defending
themselves with a weapon, they are referring to
a gun of some type and usually a hand gun.

After a great deal of research, I have changed
my mind on which is the best hand gun for defense, and have concluded that it is a .45

automatic, either the colt or the government
model. However, there are a number of words of
caution in using such a weapon.

First, a person should be well-trained in its
use and comfortable with it. There are a number
of places where one can get such training.
Probably the best known and most reputable one
is Jeff Cooper's training school at his ranch
called "Gunsight" located at:

> Box 401
> Paulden, Arizona 86334

Jeff has had among his students judges, doctors
and lawyers, as well as many high-ranking officials from foreign countries. They learn to use
this weapon effectively from all positions. He
has a room called The Playhouse where figures
pop out, both "good guys" and "bad guys." One
is taught to shoot the bad guys and not the good
guys.

The son of the head of a Latin American country
went through the training at Gunsight. A few
months later his car was curbed by a car full of
six husky youths, evidently intent upon capturing
him, killing him, or otherwise doing him harm.
After being curbed, he jumped out of his car,
rolled across the street, drawing his .45 as he
rolled, and shot all six of his attackers before
they could even get their weapons out of their
holsters.

I am not necessarily advocating this type of
self-defense in the average situation. But if
an individual is going to rely on a handgun as a
defensive tool, he needs to be able to do a similar kind of thing with proficiency; otherwise,
he would have a false security. Some people feel
a gun is their security, and when the crisis
comes, they are never able to use it.

The son of this Latin American leader was always in condition yellow, and when condition red occurred, he had preplanned his actions and could and did execute them swiftly and with precision.

SUMMARY AND CONCLUSION

Let's see where we have come thus far. Times appear to be becoming more violent. This violence can come from nature, such as volcanoes, earthquakes, tidal waves, tornadoes, hurricanes, and flooding. There are certain things one can do to prepare for these natural acts of violence, which were discussed in the last issue of MISL.

Obviously, to any intelligent observer, the acts of terrorism, hostage taking, and violent crime are on the rise in America and in the world today. One of the reasons people are susceptible to these acts of violence against their person and property is because they are in condition white too much of the time. Simply spending more time in condition yellow would allow an individual to avoid many of these situations or to nip them in the bud when they arise by simply fleeing or removing himself from the area of potential violence. For example, when one sees a large crowd gathering outside a building, it might be wise to leave the building and return at a later time after any potential demonstrations and so forth have occurred. At the American Embassy in Teheran, those who did this are not in the category of hostage today.

Another thing that people basically have not done is to develop a predetermined kind of action to take when they shift from condition yellow to condition orange or red. They need to take lessons from the pilots, the doctors, the nurses, the wise automobile drivers, and develop these predetermined plans of action.

One of the major decisions in developing a predetermined plan of action is to decide how far
you will go in protecting yourself or your property (or those persons dear to you). Once this
decision is made, it may be that appropriate
training will be necessary in order to have the
skills to follow through with your predetermined
plan of action for condition orange or condition
red.

These same four conditions could be applied to
an individual's investments. If a person would
like to invest and remain in condition white
(sleep well at night), then one should put his
investments in very long-term vehicles, such
as gold coins, silver coins, and so forth.
Those who wish to periodically move from one
investment vehicle to another are those who are
willing to be in condition yellow concerning
their investments. These are the majority of
MISL subscribers, who wish to know when the market is going to change directions so they can
take advantage of the profit potential. Those
who are day-to-day traders in the commodity
markets must, of necessity, exist in condition
orange, at least during market hours. One
would have to be here at MISL headquarters to
see the incredible amount of energy that we put
into the accounts of our money management clients. It is more than absorbing. If one does
want to trade in the commodity markets, then
one must either be willing to live several hours
a day in condition orange or pay someone to do
this for him.

Incidentally, I can conceive of no situation
where investments should take a person into
condition red. All of the suicides that came
with the stock market crash of 1929 were when
some people erroneously thought life was not
worth living without their previous financial

prosperity. This shows that they had totally neglected the spiritual side of life, which is very sad. If a person is rightly rooted and grounded in God, then no investment can ever take him into condition red or have a major physical effect on him.

We had one subscriber write in and one phone in objecting to the last issue of MISL, feeling that they wanted only financial advice in MISL. We here at MISL are concerned about the total life of our readers, primarily the financial side, but also the physical and spiritual side of life. If we see opportunities or dangers in any one of these three areas, then we feel an obligation to alert our very valued subscribers.

12

Be Prepared for
EARTHQUAKES

Reprinted from MISL #160, January 1978

Back in 1975, when MISL was first started, I wrote a
note to myself that I wanted the first issue in 1978 to
deal with the alignment of the planets. You will see
why later. Many of our subscribers may have heard of
this and even read about it, but few have seriously considered the consequences.

To summarize this situation, normally the nine planets
in the earth solar system are randomly distributed
around the sun. Once every 179 years, the planets line
up in almost a straight line on one side of the sun.
This causes a high incidence of solar flares. An increase in solar activity disrupts our radio and television communications, changes the weather dramatically
and increases earthquake activity. The planets will
line up in 1982; actually, twice that year - once in
April and once in September. However, it is estimated
that the effects of the alignment of the planets will
begin to be felt two years before 1982 and will last
two years after. Thus, the period from 1980-1984 is the
critical period.

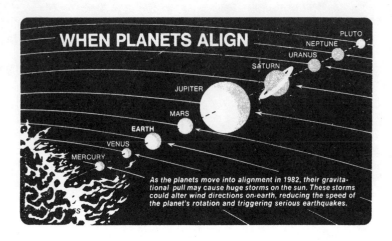

As the planets move into alignment in 1982, their gravitational pull may cause huge storms on the sun. These storms could alter wind directions on-earth, reducing the speed of the planet's rotation and triggering serious earthquakes.

Courtesy of Southwest Radio Church, Box 1144, Oklahoma City, OK 73101

In the late 1960's, John Gribbin (physical scientist editor of the *Nature* magazine) and Steven Plagemann (researcher at NASA's space center in Maryland) began to study the possible effects of the planetary alignment due in 1982, and co-authored a book about their findings entitled *The Jupiter Effect*. (Available from Survival, Inc., 24206 Crenshaw Blvd., Torrance, CA 90505. Post-paid for $2.25.) *Newsweek* summarized what these two scientists believe world conditions will be like at Christmas,1982:

1. Great increase in magnetic activity on the sun. Huge storms, sunspots and solar flares will occur.
2. The ionosphere may be seriously affected and great changes occur in the earth's atmosphere.
3. Radio and television communications will be disrupted.
4. Weird lighting effects from northern lights will burst through the sky.
5. Wind directions will be changed.
6. Rainfall and temperature patterns will be greatly altered.

7. The two scientists warn that the earth's rotation will be affected, and the length of days will be changed.

8. Solar activity in the late 50s, 60s, and 1972 has already increased the number of earthquakes and slowed down the earth's rotation, but the two astronomers warn that by 1982 *"There will be many earthquakes, large and small. . . And one region where one of the greatest fault systems lies today under a great strain, long overdue for a giant leap forward and just waiting the necessary kick, is California."*

We could spend time discussing the effects on food production brought about by the drastic weather changes. I believe that during this period we will see much less food produced than we have in the past, while our population will continue to grow. It is important to acquire *now* any food that you plan to purchase for a food storage program. As this time of alignment gets closer, the weather changes should also have significant effects in the food portion of the commodity markets.

EARTHQUAKES

Much of *The Jupiter Effect* deals with earthquakes that could be triggered by the alignment of the planets. This could be both due to increased solar activity and a tiny increase in the gravitational pull on the earth because of the planets' alignment. In the book, they state that this alignment of planets could be the final straw that triggers the massive earthquake that is long overdue in southern California. I have an academic background in geology, and would like to go back and first look at the continental plates.

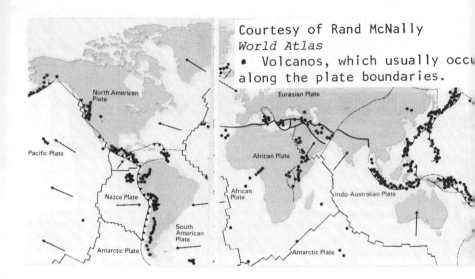

Courtesy of Rand McNally
World Atlas
• Volcanos, which usually occur
along the plate boundaries.

THE CONTINENTAL PLATES AND CALIFORNIA

When I studied geology in college, the "continental
plate drift theory" was just a theory, and few people
believed it. Today you cannot get a job teaching geology unless you subscribe to it. It proposes that all of
the land mass was once together in one place and that the
continennts have drifted apart. Most geologists today
feel that this was a gradual process - that the continents drifted apart at approximately 5 centimeters per
year. I believe that they did indeed shift apart, but
that it was a sudden movement, not a gradual one. I
will not get into my reasons for believing this, but
I would recommend reading two books. They are *Worlds
in Collision* and *Earth in Upheaval*, both by Immanuel
Velikovsky.

Most of the continents are floating on single "plates",
each of which is bigger than the continent itself. However, the North American continent is on two plates. The
majority of the United States, Canada and Alaska are all
on the North American plate, which is moving almost due
west (today at 5 centimeters per year). Baja California
and the part of California west of the San Andreas fault

are on the Pacific plate which is moving northwest, also
at 5 centimeters per year. This means that, given
enough time, Los Angeles will eventually wind up where

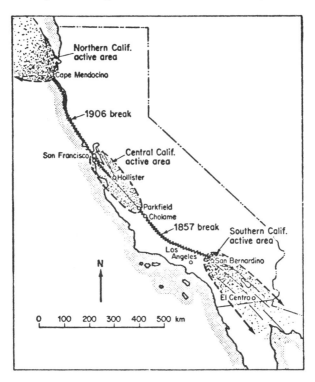

San Francisco is today. Along much of the San Andreas
fault, the plates are "creeping" past each other at 5
centimeters per year. However, because it makes a gigantic S-curve, the part around Los Angeles has been
"stuck" for several hundred years. In the book, *The
Jupiter Effect*, it is estimated that if this mass of
land were to dislodge all at once, it would move north-
ward about 40 yards. The southern California earthquake
is inevitable, although no one knows when it might happen or what might trigger it.

The Jupiter Effect puts forth the theory that the lining
up of the planets in 1982 will possibly trigger this
earthquake. This may or may not be the thing that will

actuate the southern California earthquake. It is very
likely that we will have many major earthquakes before
and after 1982 in all parts of the world. It would
therefore be wise to prepare for earthquakes. I believe that this is valid advice in whatever part of the
U.S. or the world you might live. Let us now look at
preparedness for and safety in an earthquake.

SAFETY DURING THE ACTUAL EARTHQUAKE

The big danger during an earthquake is from falling objects. Most deaths and injuries result from objects
that fall and crush or maim an individual, or from flying glass that can severely cut. The ideal place to be
when an earthquake hits is in a flat, treeless meadow.
Ground ruptures are seldom, if ever, the cause of casu-
alties. Most of the hazards are man-made. It is best
not to be under signs or poles that can snap or fall,
buildings and bridges that can collapse, or wires that
can break. Neither is it safe to be near reservoirs
and storage tanks, as they can rupture and spill their
contents.

If you are inside a house or building when an earthquake
hits, stay inside. It is best to move quickly to a position under a doorwary, in a bathroom or in a corner.
The reason for choosing these areas is that they have
extra structural reinforcement and will tend to hold up
ceilings and roofs, preventing them from collapsing on
you. It is also wise to grab a coat or blanket to put
over your head to avoid facial cuts from flying glass.

If you are outside, stay outside. Many accidents and
injuries during earthquakes occur when people are leaving or entering buildings. You should try to get out
from under things that could fall on you - telephone
and electrical poles, signs, trees and the like. Also,
the walls of buildings can fall outward during an earthquake; therefore, it is best to move to as open an area
as possible. It is likely that during the earthquake
electrical wires will be snapped and fall. It is un-

necessary to mention that you should at all cost avoid
these falling electrical wires.

Once the shaking has stopped, there will be time to
evaluate your position and plan what actions to take.
It is very likely that there will be fires (created
from broken gas lines) to be extinguished. When a
big quake hits, any or all of the following could occur:

1. The power may go off.
2. Water supplies may dribble dry.
3. Phones may be dead or tied up.
4. Sewer and gas lines may be broken.
5. Roads and freeways may be blocked by collapsed
   bridges, landslides, downed power lines, debris and stalled vehicles.
6. Fires may break out and there will be no water
   with which to put them out.
7. Police and fire services may be unable to help
   you.
8. The bottled goods in drug stores and grocery
   stores could all be smashed and unusable.

TAKE THE THREE-DAY TEST

Having been through earthquakes, I find that they hit
suddenly and without warning. One could hit your area
tonight. Would you like to find out how prepared you
are for it? I would encourage you to take the three-
day test that we have suggested before. Here is what
you do. First thing tomorrow morning, go out to the
water meter and turn off the water, go to the electrical box and throw the main switch, and go to the gas
meter and turn off the gas. Place a restriction on
your family that they can not buy anything at the drug
store, grocery store or gas station. Then plan to live
this way for three days, without making preparation.
This will show you how prepared you really are, and will
point our dramatically things that you need to do in order to be more prepared.

If you take this test, you will find that if you do not
have some water stored you will be in trouble. It might
take days to truck water to some areas after an earthquake. After the California 1971 earthquake, water in
the San Fernando valley was selling for $2 a gallon.
For drinking and cooking, allow a minimum of a half
gallon per person per day. Since there will not be
enough water to wash dishes, you will also find that
having a supply of paper cups and plates is highly
desirable.

Another discovery that you will make is that there is a
problem with waste disposal, since after one flush, the
toilet will no longer be usable. You will find that a
port-a-potty would be an invaluable asset.

Since you are reading this in the winter, heating will
also be a major consideration. If an earthquake were to
occur this winter, or some future winter, and gas lines
were broken - which would likely happen - how would you
heat? Good wood stoves would provide a valuable alternative source of heating.

Cooking is less important in that we can go up to forty
days without food, and we can sustain ourselves on un-
cooked food, if necessary. However, being able to cook
on one of the Coleman propane camp stoves, or on a wood
stove, would make survival during these times much easier and more pleasant. What would you do for lighting
if the power were off? I believe kerosene lamps to be
an essential preparation. Kerosene will store indef-
initely, and you can buy several gallon cans of it or
even a 55-gallon drum.

What would you do in the evenings during the time of
crisis following a large earthquake (or even during your
three-day trial period)? Battery-operated cassette
players and radios would provide entertainment, as would
games to play by kerosene light and books to read.
Therefore, a supply of good books and games would be a
highly desirable provision for such times.

In addition to the things that you will discover during the three-day test, there are other things that you
will want to consider having in order to be prepared for
an earthquake. A fire extinguisher is one, since during
an earthquake there would probably not be any water
pressure, which is needed to fight fires. Fire was the
big killer during the 1906 San Francisco Earthquake.

Also, do not forget to include in your first aid kit
items geared for cuts, broken bones and burns.

HOME SAFETY PREPARATION FOR EARTHQUAKES

I was in Guatemala in 1976 between the two big earthquakes. My wife and I were there a little later and
talked with people who had experienced the last quake.
The universal comment was that the noise was so deafening that it sounded like they were in the middle of a
battlefield. Can you imagine for blocks around everyone's bookcases tumbling over dumping out books, tall
China cabinets falling over, breaking all of the dishes
in them, grandfather clocks crashing over, wall units
falling and spilling their contents as well as food and
dishes flying out of the cupboards? The quake happened
at night in Guatemala. After it was over, people went
into their living rooms to find books, broken mirrors
and broken dishes strewn everywhere.

This brings us to one of the first things that we can do
in preparing our homes for an earthquake. We can put
screw eyes in the back of tall peices of furniture, and
eye screws in the studs in the walls behind them, and
wire them to the walls so that they will not topple
over. Probably the worst potential accident is the hot
water heater. During the 1971 California earthquake, a
friend's hot water heater "walked" from one side of the
garage to the other, obviously breaking the gas pipe and
water pipes that connected it. A hot water heater is
already top heavy and unstable, and is usually a prime
victim of earthquakes. The diagram below shows how
this might be cabled to the wall:

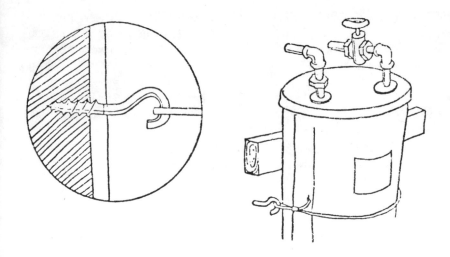

In addition, in an earthquake drawers will fly open and tend to spill their contents. Thus, positive action drawers, such as are found in most boats, would be very nice to have in a home. Since dishes will tend to fall out of cupboards, at a minimum, a screen-door-type hook could be placed on the outside of each cupboard in the kitchen, and latched when not in use. Another possibility would be to put a small piece of wood about 1 inch high inside the cupboards to form a lip, so that the dishes would not fall out even if the doors swung open.

Heavy, hanging mirrors and things of this nature will tend to come off of their hooks and crash to the floor during an earthquake. Anything that is tall and heavy, especially if it is near your bed, should be properly secured to the wall.

Most people, if they would make a complete check of their home, trying to imagine what it would be like if the Jolly Green Giant were to grab it on each side and shake it vigorously, will be able to discover things that they need to take care of in a preventative way. The way to prevent damage to your property and harm to your family is to take a little time to provide precautionary measures.

AFTER THE QUAKE IS OVER

Once the quake is over, if you are unhurt, your priorities should be:

1. To keep from getting hurt.
2. To help as best you can those who are injured.
3. To prevent further injuries and property dam-
    age.

If medical help is unavailable, do all that you can to
aid, comfort and reassure those who are hurt or frightened. Do not move injured people unless they are in immediate danger of further injury. As you go out on your
patrol to help people in need, move cautiously and wear
protective shoes. Be constantly alert for hazards that
could be magnified by aftershock.

Even a tiny spark from an electric switch, cigarette or
flame can ignite accumulated gas. Should you suspect
that there are damaged lines or possible leaks, immediately ventilate the area and turn off the gas main. *In-
door candles and open flames, such as matches and cigarette lighters, are earthquake "no-no's".* Aftershocks
may cause gas leaks, or even tip over your unattended
candles. If the fire department cannot reach you, the
smallest flame, unchecked, can touch off a neighborhood
holocaust. As far as extinguishing flames, wet towels
can be used and reused to beat out small fires, extending precious water supplies. Shoveled dirt, potted
plants, and even potato salad can be used to snuff out
flames that could destroy a house.

Fallen electrical wires can be a real hazard. To rescue
someone from wires is to seriously risk your life. A
wrong move can kill you. If you attempt such a rescue,
you must stand on dry, nonmetalic surfaces (ground,
paper, or rubber matting, and such), remaining totally
and continually insulated from both the victim and the
wires. The victim and the wires must be separated, by
pushing or pulling them apart, using only bone-dry,

nonmetalic, nonconducting objects (broomsticks, long boards, plastic pipe, and so forth).

Do not waste food. Use first defrosted food out of your refrigerator. After this is used up, begin to utilize the frozen food out of your freezer. Even if the electricity has been turned off, it still may preserve the food for several days.

Makeshift toilets must be kept thoroughly disinfected and tightly covered. Their contents should be buried deep, or kept in sealed plastic bags or trash containers along with other garbage and refuse. Keep refuse away from hungry and homeless animals that might gather around it.

Keep your transistor radio tuned in for broadcasts of conditions and emergency recommendations.

There is a real danger of an aftershock or second earthquake that can be as bad as the first. Frequently, the first big aftershock will create more damage than the initial quake, since many of the structures that have been weakened by the first shaking, will topple with the second. It has been my experience that less severe aftershocks will continue for many days after the first one or two big quake movements.

TAKE THE TIME TO PREPARE

For about $50 you can make a home fairly safe from earthquakes. A few eye screws and pieces of wire and cable will attach tall furniture and the water heater to the walls behind them. Installing hooks on cupboards, and purchasing some water storage barrels (less than $20) and a port-a-potty could make the survival of you and your family much easier during an earthquake. All it takes to make these preparations is a very little bit of money and a little time.

There are three books that I have found helpful with regard to details about how to prepare for an earthquake.

The first two are smaller - almost booklets - and the
third one is an extensive volume which even gets into
construction considerations for making new buildings
more earthquake proof. If you are interested in pursu-
ing the subject, I trust that you will find these books
useful:

> *The Earthquake Handbook*
> by Chuck Coyne
> Published by Cucamonga Press
> P.O. Box 632, Cucamonga, CA

> *Earthquake Home Preparedness*
> by Ruth Brent
> Published by DeVorss & Co., Inc.
> Box 3848, Downey, CA 90242

> *Peace of Mind in Earthquake Country*
> by Peter Yaney
> Published by Chronicle Books
> 870 Market Street, San Francisco, CA 94102

SUMMARY AND CONCLUSION

The planets are going to align on the same side of the
sun in 1982. That is a fact. The best scientific projections say that at a very minimum, we are going to
have a very significant increase in solar flares and solar activities. We know from past experience that these
do disrupt communications and have an effect on the jet
streams, rainfall, temperature and other weather conditions. Increased solar activity also tends somehow to
create an increase in earthquake activity.

We have seen that the continental plates are moving at
about 5 centimeters a year. The part of California west
of the San Andreas fault is on a different continental
plate then the rest of the United States. These are
passing by each other, but in southern California the
area around Los Angeles has been stuck for about 120
years. If that amount of land were to be moved north

about 10 yards suddenly, the impact on the earth would
be unbelievable. It could trigger dormant earthquakes
all over the United States.

I arrive at two conclusions from this. The first is the
reason that I wanted to write this article at the beginning of 1978. If anyone in southern California or any
other earthquake-prone area wishes to consider moving
his residence, he will have two years to do so before
the danger begins. I in no way want to be an alarmist
or generate fear. One has to weigh the risks, evaluate
one's own situation, and make a decision to remain or
move based on that.

The other conclusion is that it is wise to make at least
simple preparations for an earthquake, regardless of
where you live. Strapping a hot water heater to the
wall is something that requires little effort and almost
no expense. Remember, a stitch in time saves . . . maybe your life.

13

Be Prepared for

NUCLEAR WAR

Reprinted from MISL #161, February 1978

When I wrote about the Five Survivals last December, I looked at three trends that could reach a breaking point somewhere between now and the year 2000. I have had many people ask me for a more difinitive timetable for these events. Obviously, neither I nor any one else can predict when these crises are going to occur. However, we can look at periods when the probabilities are higher than normal for the occurance of an economic, political or military crisis. There is a two-year period in which the probabilities are quite high and that period is 1981-1982. There are a number of reasons for saying this, most of which are based on cycles of various kinds.

THE FOUR-YEAR STOCK MARKET CYCLE

The basic four-year stock market cycle has the stock market moving upward for two years and then down for two years, up for two and down for two. This is shown in the graph below, which was initially printed in MISL #123, in April of 1976. We can now add almost an entire additional cycle to that. 1975 and '76 were up years in the

176

stock market and 1977 and thus far 1978 have been down. As I stated in MISL #123, I believe the reason that we have the four-year stock market cycle is because we have a Presidential election every four years. If we elected a President every five years, we would have a five-year stock market cycle. In order to try to get reelected, or to leave office under conditions of prosperity, the President will do everything in his power to cause the economy and the stock market to rise during the two years prior to a Presidential election.

Since our next Presidential election is in November of 1980, I look for 1979 and 1980 to be up years for the stock market and the economy. This means that the current decline in the stock market should bottom out sometime later this year. My best "guess" would be about October, but we will have to wait and see. If this is true, at that time gold prices will peak and start down.

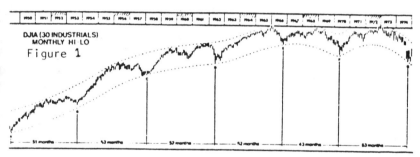

DJIA (30 INDUSTRIALS) MONTHLY HI LO
Figure 1

One of the best investment strategies, if this occurs, will probably be to move out of gold and into the stock market, but we will keep you advised on that as the time approaches.

In order to have those two up years before the Presidential election, we will see significantly higher government spending (bigger deficits) and the resultant greater inflation that will go with it. This stock market rise will tend to peak out shortly after the election and move significantly lower during 1981 and 1982. This decline could be of an orderly type such as we experienced last year and are experiencing this year. However, it could also be accompanied by panic. If panic occurs, we

get a stock market crash rather than decline. Back in
MISL #123, I presented a chart of the crisis and panic
cycles and I had this to say:

"There have been three basic overall economic and business cycles isolated. There is a 40-41 month business
cycle that was discovered by Kitchin. There is an 8-10
year (9 year) cycle observed by Juglar and a 54 year
cycle observed by the Russian scientist Kondratieff.
The composite of these is shown in Figure 2. This figure is from the book by Harry Schultz, *Panics and
Crashes and How You Can Make Money Out Of Them*, published by Dollar Growth Library. You will notice from
this figure that about 1981 all three cycles start down
simultaneously. I would consider that to be a significant danger point. It is not to say that the cycles
could not occur earlier (possibly as early as 1978) or
they could occur later. Remember, cycles do not always
occur right on schedule, but in the general vicinity of
their predicted times."

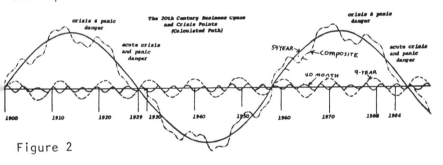

Figure 2

As you can see, way back then I was warning about the
1981 era. Everything that has occurred in the two years
since I wrote that has tended to validate this concern.
Thus, we see that 1981-1982 could be a disastrous period
in the stock market, which is one of the factors in determining that these will be crises years.

ALIGNMENT OF THE PLANETS AND FOOD PRODUCTION

In the last issue of MISL we discussed the alignment of
the planets, that will occur in 1982, and the great increase in sun spots, solar flares, and solar storms that
will result. This will have a disruptive influence on

the weather. When boiled down, it is rainfall and temperatures that will be affected. Remember that the effects of this planetary alignment will be felt for a
year or two on either side of 1982. This means that
there is a high probability that there will be decreased
food production during 1981-1982. How much decrease is
difficult to project. It could be anything from a mild
reduction in the level of production to almost no production. The consequences of lower food production
could be manifold. A moderate decline in food production would mean dramatically higher food prices. (If
you have not already stored up a year or two supply of
food, do it now before the prices go up). If the amount
of food production is extremely low, this could be the
thing that generates internal strife within the U.S.,
or international conflicts. Hungry people are desperate
people.

POTENTIAL VIOLENCE AND WAR

R. E. McMaster, Jr. has just written a book entitled
Cycles of War, The Next Six Years. In it he analyzes
the cycles of war from many aspects, such as monetary
cycles, market cycles, civilization cycles and business
cycles. It is a book well worth reading and can be ordered for $11 postpaid from:

> War Cycles Institute
> P.O. Box 1673
> Kalispell, MT 59901

Mr. McMaster points out some significant war cycles that
peak both in 1980 and 1982. He says:

"One of the most astonishing accomplishments of Dr.
Wheeler is depicted - a Drought and Civil War clock,
taken from Ellsworth Huntington's (former Yale professor) *Mainsprings of Civilization*. Notice the dates in
years around the outer edges of the clock. Immediately
inside the edge is the 170-year Civil War Cycle. The
three arcs in the interior represent the 510-year Civil
War Cycle that coincides with drought. Notice that the
intersection of the 170-year and the 510-year cycle next
occurs around 1980.

"Mr. Dewey, who heads the Foundation for the Study of Cycles, has done his own research on war as well. With regard to the 142-year cycle in war, he states, 'The 142-year pattern calls for a more than average number of battles for the seventy-one year period from 1914 to 1985. . . .' Comments on the 57-year cycle in war in 1951 include, ' . . . prudent men could not ignore the possibility that the next twenty-five or thirty years would see an increasing number of international battles.' Dewey also felt that the 1960's would be turbulent, and the middle 1970's 'reasonably peaceful.' He was right on both counts.

"Mr. Dewey and the Foundation for the Study of Cycles, in their research of Dr. Wheeler's work, discovered four recurring cyclical patterns in the Index of International Battles. The synthesis of the four cycles (142-year, 57-year, 22.14 year, and 11.2-year) corresponded very closely to actual international warfare. The next most likely time for international war is 1982, when the combined cycles peak."

LITERATURE CYCLES AND WAR

One of the cycles that Mr. McMaster examines is the cycle of American Literature. Concerning this, he says:

"Dr. David McClelland, professor of psychology at Harvard, has long had his finger on the pulse of American society, particularly as it relates to change. . . .

"One of the more interesting, yet less publicized, studies made by Dr. McClelland was presented in the January 1975, *Psychology Today*, under the title of 'Love and Power: The Psychological Signals of War.' In this article, Dr. McClelland proposed a theory of the cause of warfare that has predictive value as well.

> ' . . . the theory identifies certain motivational patterns that have typically preceded war by several years. When applied to the present, it seems to predict another American war in the near future.

Figure 3

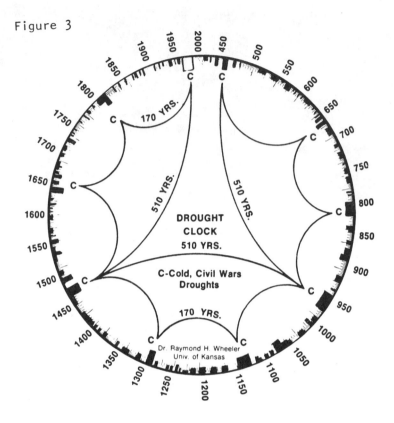

'. . . . My data points strongly to this possibility. The American people are leaning more heavily toward organized violence than at any time
since 1825.' . . .

"Dr. McClelland used three main sources of literature -
children's texts, best selling novels, and hymns in
testing his theory. The literary passages were coded
for both the need for power, and the need for affiliation. The coders had no knowledge of the hypotheses and
dates. The results were startling,

'. . . out of 13 predictions extending through
WWI, only one is incorrect. The decade of 1890
to 1900 is predicted to be peaceful, but in fact,
the Spanish American War broke out in 1898. I
doubt that this represents a serious flaw in the

forecasting ability of the model, since the Spanish American War only lasted about 10 weeks.
. . . Chance alone can hardly account for such
accuracy.'

"Using Dr. McClelland's theory, peace was correctly predicted from 1925-1935, and war from 1935-1945. A slight
degree of affiliation over power caused an erroneous
prediction for the Korean War.

"It was Dr. McClelland's opinion that Vietnam was an
exception to his predictive model. That makes sense.
How could Vietnam be the result of the reform movement
of the 1960's, since both occurred at the same time,
and many of the reformers were unalterably opposed to the
Vietnam War? Dr. McClelland believed that both Korea and
Vietnam were the last gasps of the idealism that began
in the 1930's. Vietnam was the death blow to old ideal-
istic American hopes to serve as policeman for the
world, and serve as the final arbiter of justice. It
was further Dr. McClelland's view that the reform movement of the 1960's must yet result in a war. . . .

Dr. McClelland uses periods of unrest, when the need for
power is greater than the need for affiliation, as a
predictor of war. He feels that the unrest of the '60's
must yet result in a war!

Mr. McMaster continues by saying:

"Dr. Billy Graham held an evangelistic campaign in
the Carolina's in early 1977. His opening quotes from
authorities citing the poor condition of planet Earth
were designed, as usual, to scare the hell out of his
audience. One of Dr. Graham's statements was particularly chilling. He quoted a Western European psychia-
trist who felt we were due for a major war shortly. He
stated that while on one hand people hate war, on the
other hand they become bored for war. Dr. McClelland's
work now has added predictive power.

"Later, in October 1977, Jack Mabley, in his column,
featured an article entitled, 'A Worry or A Warning.'
Mabley noted that the United States ' . . . had gotten

out of several depressions and recessions by going to war. Democratic Presidents have presided at these wars.' He brought to his reader's attention the fact that Lloyd deMause, who edits the *Journal of Psychohistory*, concluded, ' . . . the military overtones of the Carter imagery have delegated him to the role in which 'he is very likely to lead us into a new war by 1979.' ' "

KONDRATIEFF CYCLE IN WAR

In looking at the Kondratieff Cycle, Mr. McMaster says:

"Nikolai D. Kondratieff, a Russian economist and Director of the Conjuncture Institute of Moscow, in 1925 published his work on Western economic cycles. It has become popularly known as the Kondratieff Wave. Kondratieff's thesis is basically that the free world economy fluctuates in an economic cycle that peaks approximately every 54 years. He based his studies upon such items as industrial production, wages, wholesale prices, and interest rates. France, Great Britain, the Unied States, and Germany were the nations Kondratieff studied. Kondratieff actually stated that the cycle could vary between 48 and 60 years. That is logical. Cycles can extend, contract, and even sometimes disappear where human action is involved. It has been in more recent times that the Wave has been pinpointed to 54 years from peak to peak.

"In any case, the Wave runs roughly as follows: At the trough of the Wave there is a war. Then the Cycle moves up for slightly longer than 20 years. These are the good times, times of peace and prosperity. Next, there is a sharp drop off, such as occurred during 1974, followed by a plateau period of between 7-10 years. (There is also a war near the peak period.) After the plateau, it is all downhill for the next 20 years or so.

"Kondratieff is helpful in outlining the times from easy to difficult, the large swings from optimism to pessimism, from prosperity to depression, and from inflation to deflation. What is the concern here is the peak period. There is a peak approaching war (Indochina), a sharp drop off in the economy, followed by a prosperous

183

plateau, and then a depression. Most Kondratieff theo-
reticians believe the Wave peaked in 1973, dropped off
sharply in 1974, and the late 1970's is the plateau
period. Possibly so.

"The Indochina war does not prevent a subsequent war
occurring. The present Kondratieff Wave is not in keeping with the previous U.S. wholesale prices' pattern of
prior Kondratieff Waves. The divergence of U.S. wholesale prices (up) from the hypothetical Kondtarieff Wave
peak opens to thought at least the possibility that another war could occur."

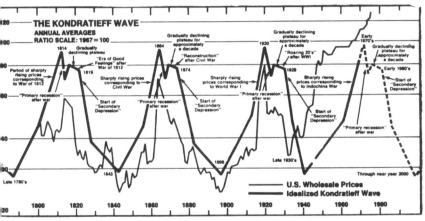

Source - International Moneyline - 1976; Media General
Financial Weekly - 1972[1]

Figure 4

OPTIMISM-PESSIMISM CYCLES AND WAR

As we all know, we as individuals, and the nation as a
whole,have cycles in which the future sometimes looks
bright, and sometimes, dismal. These cycles have been
studied in depth and can be plotted into the future. On
the graph that Mr. McMaster presents, there are three
different cycles which are combined into a composite.
The composite and two of the major cycles all turn down
in 1980, and remain negative during 1981 and 1982.

184

HUTNER'S CYCLES OF OPTIMISM & PESSIMISM

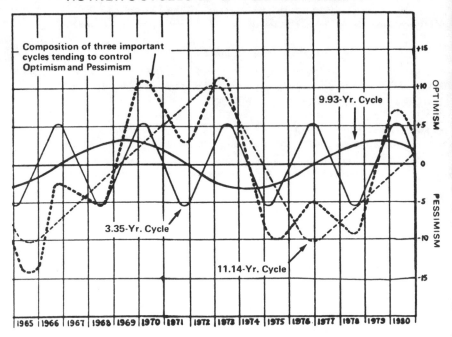

Figure 5

These cycles have been proven to be very good as predictors and Mr. McMaster comments on them as follows:

"Notice Hutner's Cycles of Optimism and Pessimism. Its
composition of the three important cycles turns down in
1980. The previous peaks, 1970 and 1973, coincided per-
fectly with the summit of the then four-year economic
cycles that preceded recessions. The 1980 crest is a
predictive bingo! It lines up with the time for violence forecast by McClelland in his earlier reviewed
literature studies. It parallels the timing of monetary
disruption and political unrest expected by Jensen and
Sauers, as well as a time of climatic instability according to Winkless and Browning. It is also when the
Kondratieff Wave's 'grace plateau' turns down. The vis-
ionaries and prophets additionally view this period as a
time of trouble.

"The evidence does not stop there! The present period
is the peak period of a number of fifty year cycles. R.
N. Elliott in his well known work, *Nature's Law*, noted a
55-year Fibonacci number cycle in commodity prices.
They inflated in 1864, 1919, and in 1973-74. Wheat, the
staff of life, runs in a 54-year cycle that has been
traced back to the 1500's. It peaked in 1974. Cycle
Sciences Corporation of San Fransicso, in their October
1, 1976, newsletter, explained that the 9-year, 18-year,
54-year, and 100-year business cycles are all headed into the pit. Bob McGregor, in a 'Special Report' prepared for the August 15, 1977 issue of *World Money Analyst*
graphically depicted the 'grand super cycle' of the U.S.
stock market from 1789 to 1975. He showed that the U.S.
stock market has been in a 'very, very long term bull
market. . .' In his opinion the market action from
1966 to the present, has, in real terms, formed a super
bull top. Last, but not least, is the 50-year cycle in
Leviticus 25 of the *Bible's* Old Testament. Israel had
seven, seven year cycles, plus one year - the year of
Jubilee, the 50th year. This 50th year brought on a
reversion of all possessions and parcels of land to the
original family owners. The implications of the Jewish
50-year cycle is that about all the debt accumulation a
society can stand prior to a major readjustment is 50
years. Also, it would seem that after 50 years, too
much wealth has been assimilated by too few, and this
must be reconciled. It has been 50 years since the
great depression."

CYCLES IN PROTECTIONISM AND WAR

Mr. McMaster has the following to say about the critical
subject of protectionism:

"Earlier in 1977 Japanese Prime Minister, Takeo Fukuda,
warned that protectionism could lead to another economic
replay similar to the 1930's. Mr. Fukuda said, ' . . .
The world economic situation following the 1973 oil crisis was quite similar to the developments of that particular time.' In the 1930's Fukuda observed, ' . . .
major countries, one after another, abandoned the open
system of protectionism.' In typical diplomatic fash-
ion, Mr. Fukuda went on to state, 'I am not suggesting
that we are once again on the road to World War. Yet I

feel deep anxiety about the social and political consequences with the world if we slide once again into protectionism, or a breakup of the world economy into trade
blocks.'

"As Ludwig von Mises put it in his economic treatise,
Human Action, 'The philosophy of protectionism is philosophy of war.' He also stated, 'If men and commodities
are prevented from crossing borderlines, why should not
the armies try to pave the way for them?'"

CYCLES OF WAR AND CAESAR

Mr. McMaster feels that the coming war will give rise to
a Caesar (dictator). He feels that Jimmy Carter has all
of the characteristics necessary for a Caesar. He has
this to say in his book:

"The natural progression of events is from a growing
democracy to imperialism. Imperialism destroys the
earlier republican institutions. Social equality comes
to the fore, and liberty lessens as the society becomes
more egalitarian. With the egalitarian tendency, increasing power accrues in the hands of one man. What is
often not understood about Caesarism is that it is not a
dictatorship, nor a clandestine grasp of power. Caesarism is demanded by the people. Caesar is loved, and is
welcome in almost all homes for dinner and a fireside
chat. It is the result of a natural progression by a
free people who no longer desire the responsibilities of
freedom, and thus turn it over to one man. The road to
Caesarism is a practical one, a pragmatic one. It is an
escape from freedom.

"Freedom is not compatible with security. Security can
best be maximized in a jail cell (maximum security) or
in a hospital. Freedom entails the assumption of risk.
The tendency of Americans to look to the government for
job security, Social Security, etc., speaks for itself.
It is evidence of a desire to avoid risk. Caesar pro-
vides security, and assumes the risk.

"Also, as has been witnessed by many political observers
in the 1970's, democratic governments are failing badly
at handling international affairs. Therefore, for all

practical matters, foreign policy is set by the White
House, the logical seat of approching Caesarism. The
'liberal' leaders in their promotion of big government,
are unconsciously taking the United States not to the
left, but to the right, where an autocratic master will
prevail. The country has almost made a complete cycle
back to the point from which the American Revolution began - a revolution for liberty against oppressive mon-
archs, and unfair taxation. Indeed, the growing tax re-
volt movement in the United States is a response to the
oppression of taxes and the tyranny of the Internal Revenue Service. . . .

"Today, the climate is right for the rise of Caesar.
All that is needed is a crisis demanding immediate decisions. The powers are already estabished in the Presi-
dency. The President has Executive Orders to be used in
an emergency. He is head of the country, the Tribune of
the People, the dictator of foreign policy, master leg-
islator, the head of his party, keeper of the economy,
leader of western civilization, and Commander-in-Chief
of the Armed Forces.

"Rome learned in the Punic and Macedonian Wars that crises in an equalitarian society demand a Caesar. The Ro-
mans descovered that in such emergencies responsibility
must be located in one man, not a congress. Grave emergencies do not allow the time for discussion, argument
and voting. The world finds itself today in a state of
permanent emergency. Such states give rise to Caesar.
Wars are the primary forerunners of Caesarism."

CYCLES OF WAR - CONCLUSION

In concluding, Mr. McMaster says:

"It is the conclusion here that the nation will be
forced to struggle with both internal conflict as well
as international war within the next six years. . . .

"Panics are the result of surprise. Will the accelera-
tion of the forces (cycles) bringing radical changes en-
gulf the masses? Just as the masses in a market expect
much higher prices at the top, so could the masses be
absolutely shocked if their lingering expectations of

good times in the future are shattered. Would a mass
surprise result in violence, internal as well as international? Can the public be warned of the potential
danger? For the reasons discussed in the Introduction,
the masses are not inclined to listen. Historically,
people resist change at all cost. Unlike members of the
animal kingdom who instinctively flee danger, man sits
around, clinging to illusions of security. Institutions
can only change slowly. Will that be satisfactory in the
near future? History says no. To think otherwise is
to ignore the unending cycles of civilizations and wars.
The flow of the tide eventually sweeps everything in its
path. The evidence gives an ominous warning.

"It may well be that during the next six years true
wealth will be measured by having plenty of food to eat,
water to drink, good health, and safe and warm living
quarters in the midst of friends and family. The cycles
say the judge with the sword is on the way."

This has been just a brief review of this outstanding
book, *Cycles of War, The Next Six Years*. I am sure that
you will want to get a copy and read the details for
yourself. But from this glimpse, we see that the probability of war in the 1981-1982 period is very high, and
should be factored into one's planning.

A NEW PRESIDENT

During 1981 and 1982, immediately following the election
of 1980, we will have a new President. If the new President is Jimmy Carter, he will have begun his final four
years and will be attempting to achieve all that he can
for the Trilateral Commission before his term ends.
This will tend to make him even bolder, since at that
point he could not be reelected, and therefore would be
less concerned about public opinion. If, like Mr.
McMaster feels, Carter does have a Caesar complex, this
would be the era in which he might try to bring about
his "permanent installation" as leader of the country.

On the other hand, if a brand new President is elected,
1981 and 1982 would be his "training years". If international mishaps were going to occur, it would be more
difficult for him to handle them, being new on the job.

This does not tend to increase one's feeling of comfort and security during this critical two-year period. This new President could also be "forced" into the status of "dictator" by world events and/or the demands of the people.

SUMMARY AND CONCLUSION

We have looked at 1981 and 1982 as potential crises years. They may not be, but the probability is high for them to be such. We are likely to see a significant run down in the stock market or perhaps even a panic and crash. We are likely to see much less food production during this two-year period, which would cause civil upheaval or possibly even an international war. In examining R.E. McMaster's book, it became evident that there is a high liklihood of international war occurring during that period. We have seen that pessimism will significantly increase during those two years, based on past cycles, producing an even greater chance of violence during crises.

Since the probability of monetary, stock market, military and economic crises occurring during 1981 and 1982 is high, we should begin now to take whatever action is necessary to get our house in order. A move toward a more self-sufficient life-style would be wise, since almost any of these crises could bring about rationing, shortages, or disruption of serivces. On the financial side of life, we will probably want to be out of paper by the end of 1980. However, there are significant profits to be made between now and then.

I hope that nothing of a crisis nature will occur during 1981-1982. However, it is best to be aware of the potential problems, and to make whatever preparations you are comfortable with, rather than being surprised and unprepared.

More on
NUCLEAR WAR

Reprinted from MISL #134, November 1976

I had not planned to do a second article on nuclear war. However, I have changed my mind for a number of reasons. First, I ran across two articles on the same subject since I wrote the last issue. There was one in the November issue of *Scientific American* entitled "Limited Nuclear War" and one in the *Plain Truth* magazine entitled "Soviets Planning to Win the Unthinkable War." Also, many of our subscribers wrote in for information on what to do in the event of a nuclear explosion. This forced me to do a great deal of research. This included reading a number of books, interviewing experts in the subject and checking the civil defense situation in the major cities in the United States. I would like to express my appreciation to my brother. R.S. McKeever, who was invaluable in both knowledge and interviewing. Our research shows that there is a vast amount of ignorance on this subject and that, unfortunately, most people's retreat preparations would do them very little good in a nuclear blast situation. Any preparations for nuclear explosions must be made *where you live*.

Therefore, I felt that I should devote one issue to briefly describing how to survive a nuclear attack. I do not claim to be an expert in this area, but am happy to pass on to you the results of my research.

I have found that there are two distinct phases involved, and different actions are required in each of the phases. The first phase is the initial blast where you have the thermal waves, the initial radiation and the wall of fire. During the second phase, the materials that were blown to fine bits in the initial explosion (earth, trees, building materials, and such), which have become miniature transmitters of radiation (alpha, beta and gamma particles), gradually float back to the earth. This is the "fallout" of the nuclear cloud that was created.

THE INITIAL BLAST

It is possible that there will be some warning of a nuclear attack. If this is so, the warning sirens will sound a steady tone for about three to five minutes and when they start warbling, this means take cover. For detailed information at that time, you should dial the emergency frequencies on your AM radios, which are 640 and 1240.

However, let's assume the worst case, where there is no prior warning. The first thing you would notice would be a very bright flash (*do not look* at the light) and, likely, an earthquake-type tremor. Within a very few seconds, you would get the blast waves and also the thermal and radiation impact. One thing to note is that these waves travel in a straight line. They do not go around corners. This means that if there was a large rock between you and the blast, these waves would go over your head if you sit in the "shadow" of the rock. The blast wave will move, at first, outward from the nuclear explosion and then, almost like the tide, come back into the vacuum that was left from the nuclear explosion. This surge out and then back could take as long as two minutes.

All is not total destruction in a nuclear blast. There
is a central area, of course, that will be totally
annihilated. However, it is interesting to note that
in the Hiroshima bomb blast, the Hiroshima Electric
Building was just one mile from Ground Zero and was
basically undamaged. In Table 1, we can see the effects of a nuclear explosion out to various distances.

Table 1
EFFECTS OF A NUCLEAR EXPLOSION
(Approximate maximum distance from explosion in miles)

Weapon Yield	Fireball Diameter	Severe Damage to Homes	Window Shattering	Paper Ignites	Second Degree Burns
20 KT*	.3	3	4	4	4
100 KT	.6	4	5	5	5
1 MT	1.4	5	9	9	10
5 MT	2.6	6	14	14	17
10 MT	3.5	8	19	23	25
20 MT	4.6	10	24	35	32
30 MT	5.5	12	27	40	40
50 MT	6.6	14	32	50	50
100 MT	9.0	17	41	65	70

KT = Kilotons (1,000 tons of TNT, equivalent)
MT = Megatons (1,000,000 tons of TNT, equivalent)
* = Size of Hiroshima bomb

As you can see from this table, even with the largest
of these nuclear devices, if you are beyond 70 miles
from the point of explosion, there will be very little
damage. Even in the larger explosions, the wall of
fire will only go out about 25 to 30 miles. In the
average nuclear device, if you are beyond 30 miles from
the point of detonation, you are in pretty good shape.
Wood will not burn from this type of fire wall. Things
such as cloth, paper and trash will, however, catch on
fire readily.

This then brings us to what you should do. If you see a nuclear flash, you should immediately "dive for cover." When the blast wave hits, it will shatter windows. There will be thousands of needle-like fragments of glass flying at very high speed. If you are at an office, crouch down behind your desk so that the desk is between you and the blast. If you are outside, dive for a ditch or lay down behind a log and shield your eyes and face. If you are at home, dive under a coffee table or bed. One of the main things to do is get away from a window because of the glass, radiation and heat that will be coming through it. The closer you are to the explosion, the less time there will be between the flash and the blast wave. Even at 30 miles, you probably only have about 20 to 30 seconds. This means that you are going to have to move and move fast.

It is also likely in a nuclear attack that they would send two missiles at each target. This means that there is possibly a second explosion coming. Therefore, once you take cover, remain there for at least two minutes. Don't try to run to another room or change position until both the outward surge and the inward surge of the blast has occurred and you are sure that there is not going to be a second explosion. Then you should have time to do a number of things and move to a shelter. Depending on your situation and the wind conditions, the fallout will probably not occur for twenty minutes to eight hours. Only a tiny percent of the people will be killed in the initial blast. The vast majority of the deaths will occur because of the subsequent fallout. That's the real danger and the one you must protect yourself from. Before looking at how to protect yourself from fallout, let's first examine exactly what fallout is.

RADIOACTIVE FALLOUT

As a result of the fireball, tiny particles of material are rapidly carried upward in the great boiling mush-

room cloud by the intense heat and upward air currents
created by the fireball. When the particles are at
70,000 to 120,000 feet, the heat in the air currents
has largely dissipated. This radioactive "cloud" is
then caught up in the prevailing winds of the stratos-
phere and is carried away from the point of detonation.
The particles of debris begin gradually to sink back
towards the earth, since they no longer have the heated
air to support them. They "fallout" of the nuclear
cloud toward the ground below. These particles range
in size from coarse grain sand down to very fine,
powdery dust. The larger particles resemble grit or
dust, while the smaller ones look like fine ashes.

Each of these particles emit three types of rays
(alpha, beta and gamma). The alpha rays can only
travel through one inch of air. The beta particles
can travel through ten feet of air, but the gamma rays
are capable of travelling one-half mile through air
and can penetrate considerable thicknesses of solid
material with ease.

Each of these particles are like a microscopic bullet.
When they pass through your body, they actually do
internal damage. If you get enough of them passing
through your body in a short period of time, your
body's natural healing processes cannot work fast
enough to heal you and, therefore, you will die. On
the other hand, you can take the same amount of particles over a longer period of time and your body's
natural healing process will have time to take effect
and handle the situation. Because of the extreme short
range of the alpha and beta particles, you do not have
to worry about them unless you actually get fallout on
your person (clothes, skin or hair). Assuming that you
take care to prevent this, the major danger then is
from the gamma radiation. Remember that the gamma rays
travel in a straight line and are stopped by approximately 2½ feet of dirt or 18 inches of concrete.
This means that, if you had a pile of gamma producing
radioactive material in one place and you had a large
pile of dirt between you and it, you could sit safely

behind the dirt. The rays would pass over your head
and around you.

Another important thing to know is the rapid rate of
the radioactive decay. About three or four days after
the explosion, the radioactivity transmission from the
particles is only about 1/100 of the level at the time
the bomb was exploded. Figure 1 shows this rapid
decay.

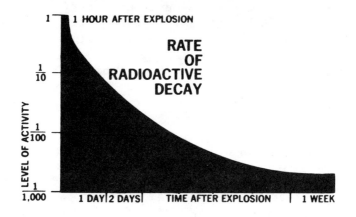

It is very important to understand the measurement of
this radiation. The basic measurement is the roentgen.
This is sometimes referred to as REM (roentgen equivalent man). Frequently, in tables or graphs, it will
be shown as "R" for an abbreviation. Table 2 shows
the effect of the total dosage of a person for both a
one week and a one month period.

DOSE (IN REMS)		EFFECT
IF DELIVERED OVER ONE WEEK	IF DELIVERED OVER ONE MONTH	
150	200	THRESHOLD FOR RADIATION ILLNESS
250	350	5 PERCENT MAY DIE
450	600	50 PERCENT MAY DIE

Figure 2 shows the number of roentgens per hour that you would receive standing in an open field at various distances from the point of the explosion. As can be seen, the winds carry the radioactivity only in one direction. But this shows that, i you were 200 miles from a blast, even downwind, you would have about 18 hours to prepare before the fallout began.

DOSE RATE CONTOURS FROM FALLOUT AT 1, 6, AND 18 HOURS AFTER A SURFACE BURST WITH FISSION YIELD IN THE MEGATON RANGE (15 MPH EFFECTIVE WIND).

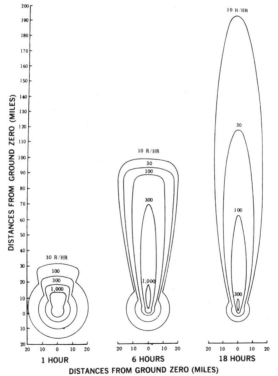

DISTANCES FROM GROUND ZERO (MILES)

A HYPOTHETICAL ATTACK

From the book *Survival Handbook* (publisher given later), we quote: "this hypothetical attack consisted of a total of 1,446 megatons of nuclear weapons yield delivery to 224 targets in the United States in the form of 263 bombs of 1, 2, 3, 8, and 10 megaton yield. Targets included 70 metropolitan areas of importance in terms of population, communications, industry, military bases, and Atomic Energy Commission installations. All the bombs were ground burst. The pattern of fallout from these hypothetical weapons bursts is shown on the maps. The fallout distribution is shown as it would be at two different times after the initial attack, illustrating the manner in which fallout spreads with the prevailing wind, covering tremendous areas of the country."

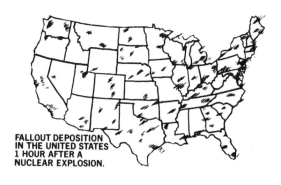

FALLOUT DEPOSITION
IN THE UNITED STATES
1 HOUR AFTER A
NUCLEAR EXPLOSION.

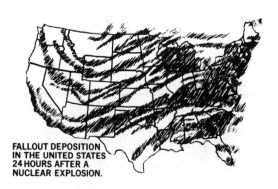

FALLOUT DEPOSITION
IN THE UNITED STATES
24 HOURS AFTER A
NUCLEAR EXPLOSION.

Another hypothetical attack was shown in the *Scientific American* article where all I.C.B.M. bases would be attacked with two one-megaton surface blasts per silo.

The Titan missiles are the white squares and the Minute-men missiles are the solid squares. The inner contour delineates a 450 roentgen dose indoors and the dotted contour represents a 200 roentgen dose indoors.

Whatever type of an attack it might be, the fallout will be downwind of the explosion and, as it falls, most of it will land on the ground and some of it on the roofs of buildings and houses. It is very important to protect against radiation from these two places. It is also important to know when the fallout is actually beginning so you can take shelter. One easy way to do this is to place a clean plate (preferably a solid pastel color) outside on each side of your house. These can be checked periodically and you will actually be able to see the fallout land on it. Once the fallout begins, it is time to immediately take shelter.

SHELTERS TO SHIELD AGAINST RADIATION

The first question is, what about the public shelters of the Civil Defense? In checking these, it was

found that they were still active; there is water
stored there. The only food stored, however, is a
cereal-based cracker. Living in a shelter like that
from 4 to 40 days could be quite a messy situation.
You would have all sorts of sociological problems -
everything from people panicking to somebody, who has
sneaked a gun into the situation, setting himself up
as a miniature dictator. Therefore, one should consider one's own family fallout shelter. My recommendation is that you do not attempt to design one of
these on your own, but use professionally designed
fallout shelters. However, if you do decide to do it
on your own, there are a number of things of which
you should be aware. To shield yourself from the
gamma rays, you would need one of the following:
approximately 2½ feet of earth, 18 inches of concrete,
3½ feet of water or 6 feet of wood. The ideal of
course is to have a shelter buried in your back yard
or built in your basement. It must have a minimum of
10 square feet per person, although an 8 foot by 12
foot shelter is usually recommended for a family of
four. Figure 5 shows a house with a basement before
and after protection is installed for fallout. It
includes things to do between the time of blast and
when fallout begins.

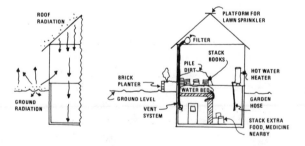

You will note that the corner of the basement where
there are no vents has been chosen for the shelter,
and a waterbed was placed on top of the shelter both
for drinking purposes and additional protection. On
top of the floor above the shelter were placed books

and anything with mass to absorb additional radiation.
It has a venting system with a hand crank, which is
necessary. The vent should be filtered. The door has
a 6 inch by 6 inch slideable opening to view outside
and to hold out your radiation rate measuring device.

Shown below are some typical family shelters. In the
back of the book *Survival Handbook* there is a list of
firms supplying or building these.

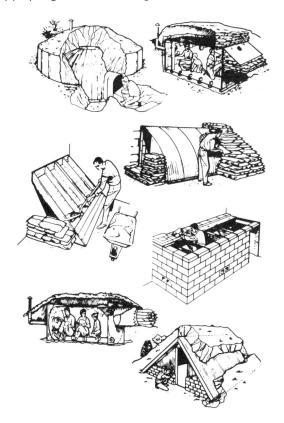

If a blast were to occur and no shelter had been provided, there is time between the blast and the fallout
to provide a makeshift shelter. If it is a home with
a basement, on the floor above where you are going to
be, you should pile books, cement blocks, bricks, and
so on. You could break open a window and shovel dirt

inside. In the basement move chests of drawers and work benches to form a rectangle. On top of this pile bags of cement, bags of fertilizer - anything with mass. If there is a vent into the basement, you could shovel dirt in from outside on top of your makeshift shelter.

For a makeshift shelter in a home without a basement, you could go in the crawl space beneath the floor and dig a hole, piling the dirt up around. This should be done in a corner where there are no vents. If you are outside and there is no way you can possibly get to a shelter area, you could drive your car over a ditch and get under it. These solutions are makeshift and rough, but it is better to lie in a hole for four days and be protected from radiation, than to go out in it and experience a sure death.

STOCKING THE SHELTER

The first and most important thing that will be needed in the shelter is water. You are going to have to oc- cupy the shelter for at least four days, and up to forty. You can go without food for four days but you can't go without water. A waterbed stored in your basement will provide a good source for drinking water. It doesn't matter if the radiation passes through it - the water is still very drinkable. When the blast oc- curs, cut off the main water valve to your house. There is enough water in the hot water heater to last. A hose should be connected to the drain valve and should run down to the fallout shelter. Do not drink water that could have fallout particles suspended in it. You must avoid ingesting fallout particles. If it is necessary to use water from a source outside where fallout has occurred, the heavier fallout particles will be at the bottom, so skim the water off of the top. Run this water through a purifier, which will re- move the radioactive particles. If this is not pos- sible,anything you can do to strain it, like running it through several layers of paper towels, will help to remove the fallout particles.

In considering food for the fallout shelter, remember that there will be *no cooking* because of the enclosed, small space and ventilation problems. This means that you are either going to have to have the survival rations like you can buy in hiking stores, or food that is already pre-cooked. Most of the dehydrated food that requires cooking will be useless in this situation. Concerning waste disposal, you can always use garbage bags for both human waste and food waste. Tie them up tightly and occasionally open the door of the shelter to set them outside. The ideal would be to have a port-a-potty or chemical toilet. Additionally, a large garbage can with a very tight fitting lid would be helpful.

Your lighting will be primarily from flashlights. After an explosion, you should have the time to gather up all the flashlights and take them to your shelter along with beds and/or bedding. Don't forget to have special provisions for babies, diabetics, and so on. Also, don't forget your radio because you are going to want to be listening to the emergency frequencies.

The first aid kit should be heavily oriented towards burns. Burns are something that you must prepare for. It is also very desirable to have some tools in the shelter. If the house or building on top were to collapse, you would need saws, axes and hammers to help work your way out. Also bring in books, games and toys for children, as well as productive, quiet things to keep everyone busy.

MEASURING DEVICES

After water, the most important things to have are two types of measuring devices. The first type is called a dosimeter. There should be at least one for each member of the family. In its most common form, it looks like an oversized fountain pen. This gives the total amount of roentgens that an individual has absorbed. The other device is a ratemeter which gives

the number of roentgens per hour that are being absorbed. Only one ratemeter per shelter is needed. I
like to compare these to the speedometer on an automobile. The ratemeter tells us how fast we are going
and the dosimeter gives the total miles we have come.
Both measuring devices are absolutely necessary. As
soon as the nuclear blast occurs, one of the first
things that should be done is to give a dosimeter to
each individual in the family. Ideally, you would have
one at the office, enough in the car for each person,
as well as an adequate number at home. It is also
necessary to have a dosimeter charger. This works on
a C battery and will recharge the dosimeter. Adequate
instructions are included with the charger so there
should be no difficulty in using it.

The ratemeter is used to determine hot spots within
the shelter. Additional protection can be piled up
in that area or, if additional protection is not possible, members of the family can rotate so that each
spends an equal amount of time in the hot spot. The
ratemeter is also necessary to determine when it is
safe to go outside. Figure 7 shows the scales on
these two devices. There will be addresses in later
sections where these measuring devices can be purchased.

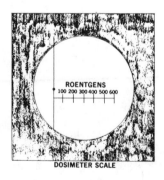

DOSIMETER SCALE

RATEMETER SCALE

LEAVING THE SHELTER

Excursions from the shelter *can* be made.   Table 3 shows
valid reasons for excursions.

Reasons for Leaving Shelter at Various
Radiation Levels

RADIATION RATE OUTSIDE THE SHELTER (r/hr)	ACCEPTABLE REASON FOR LEAVING
MORE THAN 50	Only destruction of the shelter. All other needs must be postponed at least one day.
50 TO 10	Only: a. Destruction of the shelter. b. Removal of dead. c. Severe illness, necessitating immediate treatment with medical help close by.
10 TO 2	a. Obtaining water, if very near. b. Obtaining food, if very near. c. Leaving shelter for nearby shelter with better protection factor.
2 TO 0.5	All rescue, repair, communication and decontamination work. Remain in shelter for sleeping, rest, and meals.
0.5 TO 0	Normal workday can be spent out of doors.

If the rate is 60 roentgens per hour, then a ten minute
excursion will add 10 roentgens to your personal dosimeter.

After making an excursion, it is extremely important
not to track back into the shelter any radioactive
material. Baggies could be placed over your shoes,
rain-coats could be worn, hats would be essential.
Before coming back into the shelter, all these outside
extra clothes should be removed and, ideally, the
occupant stripped and washed off thoroughly with water.
Any radiation that you track back into the shelter, of
course, will not be protected by the shelter itself,
but will be damaging to all people inside.

The canned food in your kitchen is still very good and
very usable, even though radiation may have passed
through it. It is not harmed at all. If there is any
radioactive fallout on the cans, this should be washed
off prior to their opening. At some point, it is wise
to wash off the roof of the house to eliminate the roof
radiation. If thought has been given to this situation
beforehand, a small one foot square platform could be
erected on top of the house with a lawn sprinkler on
it. Between the time of the blast and the fallout, the
garden hose could be connected to this making it easy
to wash off the roof.

After washing off the roof, the ground at the bottom
of the rain gutters will be highly radioactive. As
part of the decontamination process, this soil should
be scooped out and buried. Ground can be plowed to
bury the radioactive dust. Solid surfaces can be
washed off. Check for radioactive hot spots with the
ratemeter.

Remember that the radioactivity will probably kill most
of the animals, both wild and domestic. Protein food
will be at a premium after such a nuclear attack. Radiation does not harm garden food. Although it is
still edible, all radioactive fallout must be washed
off. New gardens can be planted, thus making a can of
survival garden seeds desirable as part of the shelter
supplies.

PLAN OF ACTION

A plan of action should be developed for your family
if you do not already have one. The following are
some suggestions for such a plan. From the time between when the blast occurs and the fallout begins:

1. Extinguish fires.
2. Turn off main water valve to house.
3. Put on dosimeters
4. Place plates outside to detect fallout.
5. Repair shelter damage, finish an incomplete
    shelter or create a makeshift shelter.
6. Move water into shelter. Connect hose to hot
    water drain and put nozzle inside shelter.
7. Move canned food from kitchen to shelter (leave
    food in freezer).
8. Take plastic garbage bags and baggies to the
    shelter.
9. Take radio to the shelter.
10. Take bedding to the shelter.
11. Take books and recreational materials to the
    shelter.

Once you are inside the shelter and the door is closed
or, if there is no door, sandbags have been placed
across the opening, you should do the following things:

1. Inventory all food and water supplies.
2. Establish a rationing procedure.
3. Appoint important tasks, such as radiation moni-
    toring and food preparation.
4. Set up schedules of eating, sleeping and daily
    tasks.
5. Establish a schedule for cranking the ventilator
    fan.
6. Begin constructive activities to occupy the minds
    of the shelter occupants, to keep them busy.

EQUIPMENT AND ADDRESSES

To purchase dosimeters or ratemeters, you can contact:

> Victoreen Instrument Company
> 10101 Woodland Avenue
> Cleveland, Ohio
> Phone: (216) 795-8200

The ratemeter is Model #493 and costs $195. Their dosimeter is Model #541-A and costs $52.50. Their dosimeter charger is Model #2000-A and costs $75. They also have a wide variety of other dosimeters in their catalog.

For the hand-cranked squirrel cage fan, used for ventilation, it can be ordered from:

> Buffalo Forge Company
> 450 Broadway
> Buffalo, New York

> or Champion Blower and Forge Company
> Harrisburg Avenue and Charlotte Street
> Lancashire, Pennsylvania

These last two addresses have been taken from books and labels on equipment. We believe they are still valid addresses, but have not yet received a response from them.

BOOKS AND INFORMATION

After having read several books, I feel there is one that is absolutely head and shoulders above everything else I have read. I think every family should have a copy. It is entitled *Survival Handbook*, by Robert C. Suggs, and covers the entire subject very, very well. It is published by the McMillan Company, New York. It is in the Library of Congress Catalog No. 62-19430. If you cannot buy a copy, it is in most public libra-

ries. The book number is 623.38-S94S. Some of the
illustrations in this article are from this book.

There are many booklets available from the Civil Defense. I understand that they are free. Their main
publication center is:

> U.S. Army AG Publications Center
> Civil Defense Branch
> 2800 Eastern Boulevard (Middle River)
> Baltimore, MD 21220

In addition, there are eight regions in the United
States designated as the civil defense regions. The
following is a list of the region headquarters from
which booklets and local information are obtainable:

> OCD Region 1
> Oak Hill Road
> Harvard, Massachusetts
>
> OCD Region 2
> Olney, Maryland
>
> OCD Region 3
> P.O. Box 108
> Thomasville, Georgia
>
> OCD Region 4
> Battle Creek, Michigan
>
> OCD Region 5
> P.O. Box 2935
> University Hill Station
> Denton, Texas
>
> OCD Region 6
> Denver Federal Center
> Building 50
> Denver, Colorado

OCD Region 7
Naval Auxiliary Air Station
Santa Rosa, California

OCD Region 8
Everett, Washington

From these, you can get a booklist and the following
booklets:

#814 "In Time of Emergency - A Citizen's Handbook on
   Nuclear Attack and Natural Disasters"
#812-1 "Home Fallout Shelters, Outside Concrete Shelter"
#812-2 "Above Ground Home Shelter"

SUMMARY AND CONCLUSION

I pray to God that none of our subscribers will ever
have to use any of the information contained in this
article. However, if a nuclear war does come, with
some knowledge and a little preparation, one can survive. Some subscribers will feel that the probability
of anything like this happening is too small to warrant
making any preparation. That's fine. But in the event
that it does occur, at least they will know what to do.
Other subscribers will feel that the probability is
high enough that they would like to pursue the matter
and make some provision, possibly acquiring dosimeters,
a ratemeter and an inexpensive shelter. Others will
feel the situation demands extensive preparation.

Whatever class you fall into, we trust that this information has been helpful.

More on
NUCLEAR WAR

Reprinted from MISL #171, July 1978

I don't believe that any thinking individual would say, as much as we would all like to, that the last war has been fought. As we look at the fighting in the Mideast, Lebanon, Southern Africa, and in Southeast Asia between Vietnam and her neighbor; the Russian buildup in Eastern Europe; and the saber rattling going on between the USA and the USSR, we must conclude that a regional or a world war is at least a possibility.

Even though we may concede that war is a possibility, it is an unpleasant one, and therefore we do not like to think about it or plan for it. If a war broke out tomorrow in one of the above-mentioned areas, what changes would you make in your investments? If you are truthful, the answer probably is, "I don't know; I've never thought about it." The purpose of this article is to cause you to think about it and to do some planning *now*.

Planning costs nothing, except some time. Unfortunately, it must always be done before a crisis occurs. For example, a wise family will have a prearranged plan as to

what each member of the family will do if their house
ever catches on fire. They may decide that the wife
would call the fire department (she will have the number
taped to the phone), and the husband would run for the
garden hose and do what he could to arrest the fire. The
children would go immediately to the garage and wait for
their mother to join them after she has completed the
phone call. A fire plan could be that simple. However,
if no planning were done beforehand, and fire were to
break out, everybody would jump up shouting directions
at one another, and there would tend to be mass confusion. I believe that it is well, even after you have
thought out such a plan, to have a "fire drill" about
once every six months, just to be sure that everyone
knows what to do. One of the parents could call such a
drill just as dinner was finishing some evening.

Just as it is wise to have a prethought-out fire action
plan, in order to avoid confusion and panicky decisions
at the time a fire occurs (even though we hope it
doesn't), I believe that it is also wise to have a pre-
thought-out plan as to what to do in your investments,
in the event that a war breaks out in some area in the
world, also to avoid confusion and hasty decisions at
such a time.

Incidentally, I hope that this article will be a short
one, so that I can include some of the items that I have
been collecting concerning what others are thinking about
the potential of war.

MIDEAST WAR

As much as the U.S. is trying to bring about peace in the
Mideast, and trying to play both sides against the middle, it still looks as if war there could be an imminent
possibility. In commenting on the fighting in Lebanon,
Friday, July 7, *The Wall Street Journal* said:

"Israel warned it might intervene in the escalating
fighting in Lebanon.

"Israeli warplanes roared over Beirut in what U.S. officials saw as a signal that Israel stands ready to help
the Lebanese Christian militiamen against Syria. A
spokesman in Jerusalem said the Syrian siege of the
Christian sector in Beirut was resulting in a 'massacre'
and that Israel wouldn't let the Christian forces be
'annihilated.' The Christian militia has aided Israel
in the fight against Palestinian guerrillas in southern
Lebanon. In Washington, the administration started a
crash diplomatic effort to stop the six-day-old battle.
Washington was especially concerned about Lebanese President Elias Sarkis' threat to resign, which would create
an even greater power vacuum.

"U.S. officials also are worried that an outbreak of
fighting between Syria and Israel, which are old
foes, could wreck the Egyptian-Israel talks sched-
uled for this month in London.

"President Carter called for a cease-fire, saying the
fighting was causing suffering to innocent civil-
ians. . . ."

Let's say you woke up one morning to the news that Israel
was at war with most or all of its Arabian neighbors.
What should you do? Some of the physical preparations
that we have recommended, hopefully you would have
already completed. These would include such things as:

1. Having a 500-gallon gasoline tank installed at
    your home, which the gas company would fill
    monthly, to supply the gasoline for your vehi-
    cles

2. Buying a small car that has very good gas milage

3. Becoming very good friends with you local gas
    station attendant (taking him cookies from the
    wife, etc.)

These are but a sample of the things that we have recommended in various issues of MISL. If you haven't done them before such a war occurs it might be wise to do them just as soon as major fighting breaks out. This is not to say that there definitely *will* be an oil embargo, but at least one should be prepared for such an occurrence.

Turning to investments, it is wise to look at what changes we could make in order to profit from the hostilities. I won't get into the morality of profit from a war, but will simply say that *someone* is definitely going to profit, and you have to decide whether or not you are going to be in that group.

If you are a commodity trader, there is an interesting spread that proved to be very profitable during the last oil embargo. The glue for plywood comes from petroleum. Therefore the spread of going long plywood and short lumber worked out very well. That is, the value of the plywood in relation to lumber increased.

Regarding the currency situation, with Mexico developing as a significant oil producer, an oil embargo from the Middle East should strengthen the Mexican peso. Therefore, I would go long on the IMM Mexican peso futures. (I'm aware of the trauma caused by the Mexican peso devaluation, but it has been performing nicely in recent months.)

Concerning the stock market, if there is an oil embargo, the prices of the stocks of companies that use petroleum in their products will tend to drop. Some examples of heavy petroleum users are paint manufacturing companies, fertilizer producing companies, and chemical companies. The rationale behind the drop is that the cost of the raw material will go up while the price of the products will not go up as much. This means that the company's earnings will be down. This may or may not be correct thinking, but that is the thinking that I believe the mass of public investors will tend to use. Conversely, people will tend to think that the oil companies are going to make more profit and consequently, even if on a temporary basis, the price of the oil company stocks will tend to go up.

Let me put these suggestions into a proper perspective. I am not suggesting that what I have mentioned above should be *your* investment changes, if there is a Mideast war. What I am suggesting is that you think through the consequences of such a war, as you would see them, and write down *your own personal plan*. Some of my thoughts may be helpful and beneficial to you in formulating your plan. Maybe you will want to talk to others, whose investment knowledge you respect, to help you come up with a written plan, customized for you and your situation.

WAR IN SOUTHERN AFRICA

When I raise the possibility of war in southern Africa, you may think: "You've got to be kidding, Jim. Angola, Zaire, South-West Africa, Rhodesia and so on are already a hotbed of one war after another." This is true, but what we are looking at here is a serious invasion of Rhodesia and/or South Africa. If Rhodesia goes, basically so goes the free world's supply of chrome. Rhodesia and Russia produce almost all of the chrome in the world. You may think that chrome is unimportant - that we could do without shiny bumpers on our automobiles. That is true. However, chrome is essential in making steel. If the free world loses Rhodesian chrome, the steel making companies could be affected in the same way as the paint producing companies in the case of an oil embargo. The cost of chrome could skyrocket or, in times of real tension with Russia, it could become unavailable, if Rhodesia falls into Communist hands. Therefore, the price of the stock in the steel-producing companies would likely decline.

If South Africa were to go Communist, it would be even more significant, since they produce:

    75% of the world's gold
    85% of the world's diamonds
    50% of the world's uranium

If South Africa were to fall into Communist hands, the prices of these three commodities would skyrocket.

South African gold shares on the other hand, with an invasion of South Africa, could plummet to almost zero value. With a war going on, the mines would likely come to a halt in production and could even experience sabotage. South African gold shares are no longer the comfortable, "keep ahead of inflation and earn 10% a year" kind of investment. They are now a high risk investment and should be treated accordingly. This means that if you are going to have a higher risk, you need to have a higher rate of return for it to be an attractive investment. Thus, for now, I would recommend dealing only in the precious metal and not with South African gold shares.

These are but some thoughts on a serious threat of war involving Rhodesia and/or South Africa. Each investor should think through for himself what he feels the consequences would be and write down a plan of what to do if war were to break out involving either of these two countries. Also the timing is important. Does one make investment adjustments the day after the war starts or does one try to anticipate it? This question of timing is, of course, an individual decision, but as these things appear imminent, we will try to keep you posted in MISL.

WAR IN EUROPE

As we have reported in MISL, there is an enormous build-up of Russian military strength in east Europe. Most of the free world military experts agree that Russia could take all of Europe in roughly 48 hours, if they started a concentrated push. This posture of strength has been recently aided by Jimmy Carter's decision not to deploy the Neutron bomb.

If Russia were to take over Europe (remember, I am saying *if* they do; I am not suggesting they *will*), I do not

think that Switzerland would be spared, as was true in
the case of Germany during World War II. If the Commun-
ists come into a country, take over all of the land and
distribute it to the "needy", what makes you think that
they would not take all of the wealth stored in Switzerland by the "rich capitalists" and distribute it to
whomever?

This brings us head on into a subject I would like to
avoid - that of Swiss bank accounts. I have and still
do, recommend having a Swiss bank account and having a
portion of your wealth stored there. That is good advice for now. It may not be good advice if a military
conflict looks imminent in Europe. If a war starts
there, I would bring everything home from Switzerland,
in U.S. dollars.

There are two types of money that people place in
Switzerland. One is legitimate money, on which taxes
have been paid, and the other is gray money consisting of
funds that have not been accounted for to the IRS. (I'm
against having gray money, but since some of out subscribers have some there, we need to address their situation.)

If you are a person with both legitimate funds in Switzerland and gray funds, I would suggest having two separate accounts in two separate banks. If a war were to
break out, bring home the legitimate funds immediately.
If you have prearranged with your Swiss bank, it is possible that they will loan you money (U.S. dollars), using your gray funds account as collateral. If this is
something that you think you might wish to do, arrange-
ments must be made well ahead of time. If you do bring
any of these funds home and a threat of war or war itself ceases, and Switzerland proves to remain a haven,
they could be returned quite easily.

If it is your intention to bring home such funds, I
would suggest that as part of your written planning you
write out the cable (or wire) that you intend to send

with the account numbers and so forth, so that if anything does happen, without having to scramble around looking for account numbers, you can immediately phone in the cable. Remember "first come, first served", and they are going to get a flood of cables following yours.

Looking at the commodity market, the European currencies - Swiss franc, Deutsche mark, Dutch guilder and French franc - will all plummet, in the event of a European war. Thus, immediate short positions should be taken, if they do not open limit down. In this area, it will probably be necessary to do a little anticipating. When the hostilities seem to be imminent, short positions should be taken. Gold and silver should move up in this scenario.

There may be other types of investments that one could make, but would not normally consider. For example, if Russia were to take over Europe, the supply of Swiss watches to the free world could likely be stopped. If war were to break out in Europe, one could buy a supply of new Swiss watches, which should appreciate significantly in value. There may be other items manufactured in Europe that one could also acquire a supply of. However, one would not want to buy say, Volks Wagons, because even though they are "German", most of them are made here in the United States. Some of the other European cars, such as a Porsche, might indeed appreciate in value because of the cut off in supply. In these areas, one would have to do some homework and be sure of his ground before making a substantial investment. On the other hand, if one wanted to buy a Porsche or Swiss watch for one's personal use, the time to buy it would be the day hostilities broke out in Europe.

WHAT ABOUT A WORLD WAR?

As we begin to consider a world war, we first need to look at the possibility or probability of it occuring. I would like to draw your attention to the section in

this issue of MISL entitled "What Others Say". There
we have included a number of items on this subject, by
various publications.

I believe that we are heading for a showdown between
the two major powers. What form it will take is yet to
be seen. The U.S. could simply surrender and never face
a confrontation, the U.S. could gradually acquiesce to
every Soviet demand and slowly become Communist, or there
could be a breakout of hostilities between the two major
powers. (Possibly with Red China on the side of the
U.S.) If there is actual warfare, it could either be a
nuclear war or a conventional war.

If there is a conventional war, a number of things are
likely to occur. We could have price controls followed
by shortages. For our new subscribers, we had two issues
dealing with this. Issue #140 was entitled "Price Controls Cause Shortages" and issue #141 was "Prospering
During Price Controls". (These two issues together are
available for $5, if you missed them).

To protect yourselves against shortages, you are going to
want to have a supply of hard, tangible items and to be
out of paper. You would want to have a supply of food,
automobile tires, batteries and other auto parts, materials for your business, gasoline, nails, pipe - anything
that is likely to be in shortage that you will need or
can sell later for a significant profit. Gold and silver
should do quite well in this time and the price should
escalate very rapidly.

On the other hand, if there is a nuclear war, we are in
somewhat of a different ballgame. Hopefully you will
have made at least some of the preparations we outlined
in MISL #135, "You Can Survive a Nuclear Attack." If you
missed that issue I would suggest that you get my book
instead, since it contains the contents of that issue
with some additions.

Assuming that you survive the nuclear holocaust, that a

number of cities and manufacturing facilities have been destroyed, but that we still exist as a nation, again you would want to have supplies of hard, tangible items such as food, automobile parts, materials for your business, and so forth - anything liable to be in shortage. However, in this scenario, I would be much less excited about gold and silver. I would rather have the emphasis on useable, tangible items.

Hopefully, you will have a written plan as to what each member of the family should do in the case of a nuclear attack. My book gives some detailed suggestions on this that might be helpful, if you have not already made preparations. Also, if there is any warning and you have time to prepare, an investment shift, out of anything that is paper and 100% into hard, tangible items, I believe would be wise. You may or may not agree with that. That is fine. I do suggest, though, that you think through what changes you will make if you see a world war coming and record those actions so that you have a pre-thought-out plan.

Although war is an unpleasant subject to contemplate, most thinking people agree that it is at least a possibility within the next few years. Others, like R.E. McMaster, as advanced in his book *Cycles of War*, feel that it is almost inevitable. However you feel about war, there is at least enough likelihood of its occurrence that you should take a few minutes to formulate and record your strategy of both investment and physical changes that you would like to make if war broke out in one of these areas. This planning costs no money; it requires only a little bit of your time. But just as with a plan of action for your family in case your house catches on fire, it could be very valuable, when the time comes, in order to avoid confusion and irrational decisions.

I pray with you that war will be avoided, in the same way that I would pray that neither your house nor mine burns down. However, planning for an emergnecy situation is the better part of wisdom.

14

Be Prepared For
COUNTRY LIVING

Reprinted from MISL #164, March 1978

My thinking has changed on a very vital subject and I feel an obligation to pass this on to you, our valued MISL subscribers. On the subject of retreating, I NO LONGER feel that:

1. Commercial group retreats
2. Retreating on wheels
3. Retreating on a boat
4. An isolated wilderness cabin

are viable alternatives for retreating. Before discussing why I do not believe these are viable alternatives, and which approach I now recommend, we should first examine the whys and wherefores of retreating.

THE FUTURE OF BIG CITIES

Those of our subscribers who live in large cities know down inside that cities are becoming progressively undesirable as a place to live. Yet many people feel that

222

they are "trapped" in the city. I believe that this notion is unfounded, and we will see why I say this. If nothing else, air polution alone makes a city an undesirable place to live. The air that people breathe in a city has got to affect their overall health, energy and stamina. We recently had a couple from a city visit us here on the ranch. They commented a number of times, "I had forgotten how sweet air can smell."

As the probability of a nuclear war continues to increase - and we will have more to say about that in this issue - the large cities are obviously some of the prime targets for enemy nuclear war hits.

There could also be a disruption of the fragile food distribution systems and a breakdown of serivces. This could come with an economic collapse (the dollar becoming worthless), since people would not go to work for worthless money. If the firemen did not go to work, there would be no fire protection; if the policemen did not go to work, there would be no law and order; if the truckers did not go to work, there would be no food in the stores; if the people in the water department did not go to work, water would soon give out, and on and on. These services could also be disrupted because of terrorists blowing up electrical and water distribution plants. As we have seen in the recent New York blackout, a disruption of these services, in today's world, tends to generate looting and rioting.

For years many people have realized, many initially through Harry Browne's writings, that if such a mess were to occur in a city, they would want a place out away from the city to which they could go for a period of a few days or even a few years until the cities again (if ever) became a desirable place in which to live.

In times past, I have recommended various methods of retreating, most of which I can no longer recommend with a clear conscience.

HOW NOT TO RETREAT

As I mentioned earlier, I can no longer, with a clear
conscience, recommend a commercial group retreat. In
most of these there is a single central building or two
constructed, and nothing on the individual "lots" for
the retreaters. If everyone dashed to a place like that
at the last minute, with campers, tents or trailers, it
would look like a Palestinian refugee camp. The only
basic food the people would have would be what they
brought with them. There would be no permanent sanita-
tion facility for a crowd that big, and there would be
difficulty as to how decisions would be made for the
group, which is one of the key factors. However, an
even more important factor is the mix of skills and tal-
ents that would occur. In most commercial group retreats that I have seen, you would have 50 doctors, 3
lawyers and no one to do any work. The skill mix would
be a major problem, even if each person were required to
build a permanent structure on his group retreat "lot" and
to stock it with a year's supply of food. In a "thrown
together" artificial community, it would be essentially
impossible to have a complementary balance of basic
skills.

Some writers have recommended "retreating on wheels".
In this approach you would hop into your camper, pull
behind it a trailer loaded with dehydrated food and
equipment, and take off from the city to wander the
courtryside. If the cities remain uninhabitable for a
period of years, within six months to a year, someone
retreating on wheels would either become one of the
looters or would become a squatter someplace. This does
not seem to be a desirable or workable alternative.
Others have recommended retreating on a boat. Having
lived on Catalina Island and having been around the
ocean much of my life, I love to sail, and enjoy power
boats (smudge pots) as well, although not as much. Being very fond of boats, I can see how the owner of a
boat would be strongly attracted to this approach to retreating. However, there are two significant negatives

to this approach which would cause me to avoid it. The
first is pirates. Imagine that things really went to
total anarchy and you took off in your trimaran (which
is the best boat for retreating), with the outer hulls
loaded with food and supplies and the center hull re-
served for living quarters. On board were your wife
and your children. After a few days, along of you comes
a big power boat with 10 or 12 burly guys on it saying
"Pull over, we are coming aboard." What do you do? If
they intend to steal your food and rape your wife, how
do you protect yourself? If you were to take this approach, you would need a weapon capable of blowing a 6-
inch hole at the water line of such a pirate vessel. A
weapon of that caliber is illegal to own and therefore
you are stuck. The other problem is what happens when
you run out of supplies? You would need to have a cove
somewhere where you had additional food stashed and a
supply of fresh water. If you are going to go to all the
trouble of having a cache of food stored and developing
a fresh water supply, that time and energy could better
be spent developing a more viable retreating alternative.

The isolated cabin way out in the wilderness is undesirable for a large number of reasons. One is the avail-
ability of help in times of medical or other emergencies. There are also times when there are things too
heavy for one man or one family to do, such as raising a
barn roof. One needs neighbors who can help one another
with these types of tasks. Also, such an isolated cabin
would be totally vulnerable to attack by intruders. If
you had to have a "watchman" on lookout at all times, it
could tremendously disrupt your family and in general
create such fatigue and tension that it would become an
intolerable situation. I would also dissuade anyone
considering a cabin at a ski area, or any other resort
area, as a retreat. Any affluent area like that will be
a prime target for looters. Also, you have an economic
system at the resort that is dependent almost totally on
the affluent spending paper dollars. If that spending
were to cease, such a community would fall apart in a

hurry. With all of the resort employees out of work
and hungry, what would happen? Most resorts do not produce their own food and are totally dependent on the in-
coming trucks.

A SMALL RURAL TOWN IS THE BEST ALTERNATIVE

In discussing this matter with a number of other survival experts, such as Bill Pier, owner of Survival, Inc. and
Mel Tappan, editor of *Personal Survival Letter*, we have
all independently come to the same conclusion: that is,
that a small rural town is the best retreating alternative. I appreciate the inputs of these men for this article. Incidentally, *Personal Survival Letter* deals entirely with physical survival. If you are interested,
you can subscribe by sending the $100 annual subscrip-
tion fee (for 12 issues) to:

    P.O. Box 598
    Rogue River, OR 97537

There are a number of reasons for a small rural town being the most desirable alternative. One of the first
ones is that there is already the right mix of skills
and talent. There is a doctor, a plumber, an auto mech-
anic, barbers, grocery store operators, and so on. All
of the basic supplies for these various people in their
trades exist there. They are usually a cohesive unit,
since, in a sense, they take care of each other. The
first step is to locate a small town that you think
would fit your purposes. After you have done this,
look for a specific piece of property near that town.
Since the first step is to locate the right town, here
are some of the characteristics that I feel are important:

_____ 1. 2,000 to 39,000 population.

_____ 2. Not closer than 300 miles to a major city.

226

_____ 3. Not on a major highway.

_____ 4. All basic services exist there.

_____ 5. At least one doctor resides there.

_____ 6. Preferably there is a hospital.

_____ 7. No ghettos.

_____ 8. No racial problems or potential ones.

_____ 9. No religious problems.

_____10. Good climate (rainfall, and growing season).

_____11. Not flood prone.

_____12. Minimal danger of nuclear fallout. (See MISL #135)

_____13. Not a resort or college town.

_____14. Produces its own food supply.

_____15. Not economically dependent on anything other than small farms.

_____16. Not right on the coast (danger from tidal waves).

_____17. Not earthquake prone.

_____18. Has a good library.

_____19. Has good schools.

_____20. Citizens are of good character and hardworking.

It is unlikely that you will find all of these characteristics in most towns. However, if the town you are considering misses on more than one of these, I would skip it because there are towns that do meet all of these criteria.

I might say just a word about a few of these, where it may not be intuitively obvious. In the upcoming social upheaval in the U.S., I believe some of the major tensions will be between races. Therefore, I would recommend that you look very carefully to be sure that the racial situation would not be a problem.

I would not want a small town that had one large industry, such as an IBM plant. If that plant were to close down, huge numbers of people would be out of work. Similarly, you would not want an area with vast numbers of welfare recipients. In the event that their welfare payments were suddenly cut off, they could become an angry bunch to contend with.

Personally, I would prefer a town large enough to have a good hospital. It is good to have a doctor, but at times you also need operating and X-ray equipment that a doctor would not have in his home. This would require at a minimun, either a very large clinic that had this equipment, or a small hospital.

To me the church situation is very important. If you place high value on the spiritual side of life, you would want to be sure that there are groups of people with whom you were spiritually compatible. This would mean spending a couple of Sundays (or Saturdays, if you are Jewish or Seventh-Day Adventist) in a town visiting the various churches or synagogues to be sure that you are comfortable with the spiritual life there. You may also want to be careful about moving into a town that is predominantly of one religion, in which you would be of a significant minority. As much as I love my Latter Day Saint friends, and my Southern Baptist friends, I'm not sure that I would recommend that a Southern Baptist move into a town in Utah where everyone else was LDS. Conversely, an LDS may not be comfortable moving into a Southern town where he was the only LDS in the entire town. (I in no way mean to pick on these two; I am just using this as an example.)

The town should be in an area that produces its own food supply. This means that there would be orchards, grain fields, cattle being raised, an so on. Some areas in the Midwest that raise nothing but grain, I do not consider as having their own self-sufficient food supply.

One other item of significance is the character of the people. Some small towns are dead and lethargic; a group of rioters could come in and take them over without a whimper. In other small towns, the people are hardworking, have drive and have a sense of territorial imperative. They have worked hard for what is theirs and they intend to hang onto it. I would also be concerned about the general morality of the town.

Once you have found the right small town, it becomes a matter of finding the right piece of property for. your family in or near that town. Assuming that you want to grow your own food, this means that you are going to be looking for at least 5 acres. (You can survive quite nicely on 5 acres.)

WHAT TO LOOK FOR IN A FARM

The three most important things to look for are water, water and water. This is not only a water supply for the house, but also for growing gardens, grains and hay. In most places in the country these all require irrigation. It is not enough to have a stream or river flowing through or by your property. You have to know that it is flowing year-round and that you can take out of it all of the water that you need. The most desirable, in my opinion, is a spring higher up than the house, which feeds the house and the garden by gravity. Wells are less desirable since they require a pump of some type. Today most pumps are electric and if your electricity supply is cut off, so is your water. If this is the case and it is of concern to you, you may need to put in a windmill which would pump water up to a holding tank which would gravity feed water to your house and garden. Since a 35-foot high tower for a water tank could be quite expensive, this probably implies that you are not going to want a flat piece of property.

After water, the next most important thing is soil. Unless the water supply is there, you don't even need to worry about the soil. If you do have an adequate water supply, then have the soil tested to be sure that it will produce the things that you want to produce.

After these two items, everything else is up to subjective judgement. Usually if a property is fenced and has barns and other outbuildings on it, it is a good deal because you could not put in those improvements for what you will be paying for them. As we discussed in MISL #154, if there is a house on the property, you can be sure that you will remodel it. In the city you buy the house and take the land that goes with it. In the country, you buy the land and take the house that goes with it. Therefore, I would rather buy a place without a house on it. It's almost easier to build from scratch than to make major remodeling changes.

This takes us to the various approaches you could take in becoming part of a small community.

APPROACHES TO BECOMING A COUNTRY BOY

The best approach by far is to find the right town, find the right piece of property and move there NOW. I will now make a categorical statement: ANYONE can move to a small town now. It is simply a matter of priorities, volition, standard of living, and so forth. I know of a man who had a highly specialized job in the space program. He said that he could not move to a small town because there would be no work for him. Mel Tappan asked him if he had a hobby that he enjoyed. It turned out that he very much enjoyed tying flies for fly casting. He moved to a small town, started a business tying flies and today is making $30,000 a year tying flies. I recently had a dentist write me and say that it would be impossible for him to move to a small town. When I read that, my internal reaction was "baloney". There are many small towns that really need a dentist. True, he may not have a $100,000-a-year practice. It may drop down to $20,000 a year. But that is a choice that each one of us has to make. Almost every one of our subscribers are of the caliber that if they were to move to a small town, within six months they could have purchased a business, started a business or in some way be making a living that would meet their basic needs.

I realize that some people are two years away from retirement with their current company. Moving immediately may be difficult for them. (Although they *could* move.) There are a number of approaches that they could take. They could find and buy a 5- to 10-acre piece of property. Let's assume for a minute that it had one house on it. They could rent this out to a caretaker family so that the property would be secure. They could then plant an orchard and leisurely begin building a second house on the property for their own residence. This means that they would become involved with the local contractors and become known in the community. They could then use the second house as their vacation place and spend some of their weekends there, until such time as they could move there permanently.

Another alternative, but less desirable in my eyes, would be to buy the acreage without a house, put in a well and a septic tank, and plant the orchard. If you never utilize the property for yourself, it is going to appreciate as the fruit trees mature. Even a barn could be added in which some of the basic equipment needed for the garden and the fruit trees could be stored.

The advantage of any of these approaches is that you get to know the people in the town and you are not the "stranger" who zoomed in at the last minute before the crash. Another advantage of moving there now is that there is a lot of experimenting that you need to do and many experiences that you need to have in order to gain the knowledge to produce your own food. You need to experiment with goats, hogs and chickens to find out which ones you like, and which ones are more trouble than they are worth. You need to know when to plant and how to prepare the soil. One of the keys is the irrigation system. There is no way that you will ever get that right the first year. Add to this the peace of mind, the fresh air and the relaxed pleasant way of life, and you can see why I would strongly recommend moving now.

I bought a whole host of books when beginning to look for property. There were two that were by far the most helpful ones. They are:

> *First-Time Farmer's Guide* $4.95
> by Bill Kaysing
>
> *Farming for Self-Sufficiency* $7.50
> by John and Sally Seymour

These can both be ordered from:

> Survival Inc.
> 24206 Crenshaw Blvd.
> Torrance, CA 90505

You should add 50 cents per book for postage and handling.

THANK GOD I'M A COUNTRY BOY

As soon as you move back to the country, you are going to feel the same way. There are many new things to learn and they are all fun and exciting. Even the mistakes are fun. You will enjoy turning up the soil, planting seeds and watching them grow to produce edible food; raising a bunch of baby chicks to frying size and then taking a day to kill and dress 20 of them to put in your freezer; and knowing that the food you are eating you worked to produce with your own hands. There is a sense of independence, health and vigor that one just cannot get living in the city.

If you really are concerned about making a living, in towns that have 30,000-39,000 population, there are many businesses that come up for sale, and many others that need to be started. If you are good with gardening and trees, maybe starting a nursery is the thing. If you are good with mechanical things, maybe starting a tractor sales agency of one of the new Japanese four-wheel drive diesel tractors is for you. Maybe a business in solar energy, hydroponics, and wind and water energy is needed. Perhaps there is something else that you have longed to do, and are good at, and this would be the opportunity to do it. It has been proven that if you do what you enjoy, you will succeed at it and prosper.

Back when I had a Young Life Club and counseled with many high school seniors about their future, I always asked them this question: "If I would guarantee you an income of $5,000 per month for life with the provision that you had to work at something, what would you do?" The answer to that question always told me what they enjoyed doing. If they said doing oil paintings, being a nurse, repairing cars, or teaching children, that was the thing that they would really enjoy doing. If they did what they enjoyed, they would not only have a fulfilling life but I believe a very successful one. There may be something in a small town that you would really enjoy doing even if it means switching fields (no pun intended) and it could also prove to be quite productive for you.

THE TIMING OF THE MOVE

I do not think that we are going to go to sleep one

night and wake up the next morning to major riots in the city. I think that this could be a gradual thing that will progresseively get a little worse and a little worse. About the only thing that I can see happening suddenly would be an earthquake or a nuclear attack. However, I should remind you of the story of the frog, that I have used before. If you drop a frog into boiling water he'll jump out. If you put a frog in cool water and put it on the stove, he will sit there and be slowly boiled to death. I think that most people are going to be like the second frog: they will keep waiting, thinking that things will get better again. They will wait and wait until it is too late.

The attitude that many people have had - that of waiting until things get really bad and then dashing off to a retreat - I believe is both dangerous and unworkable. What that really means is that you would have to leave your home and all its furnishings, your job, all that you have to the mercy of whoever remains behind in the city. It would be extremely difficult to make such a decision because if you were wrong, then you would have to go back, and it would be even harder to make the decision to leave the next time things looked warningly bad. What we are talking about in this article is carefully thinking it through, finding a piece of property, moving your residence NOW to a small town and finding or developing a way to make a living in that small town. The couple who own the general store out in our area are from California. They bought the general store from an old-timer who, I assume, wanted to retire. They are living very happily and enjoying it very much. Almost any of our subscribers, whether you be a doctor, lawyer, engineer or accountant, would be capable of buying and operating a general store. Some may consider it "beneath them" but the drop in status may be well compensated by the gains in health, peace of mind, freedom and so forth. Think it over. It may not be for you. On the other hand, it might be.

HOW MUCH TIME DO WE HAVE? *Gary North's Remnant Review*

Doctor Gary North, in his March 17, 1978, issue of
Remnant Review (713 W. Cornwallis Rd., Suite 100, Durham, NC 27707), discussed this question beautifully. He
said:

"It is indicative of the present moral, political, and
economic disruptions that the West faces that people are
seriously asking this question of themselves and of
others who are supposed to know the answer. Not that
many people are seriously asking it, of course. That
kind of question is limited to those who have something
to lose and who are convinced that the present drift of
world events can lead only to a situation which threat-
ens everything they have built up over the years.
Thoughtful people who have both capital and a sense of
history are clearly in a minority in any period. They
are no less a minority today.

"Nevertheless, the question seems to demand an answer.
People ask me this question several times a week. The
question is almost, though not always, rhetorical. It
is prefaced with some observations. They run along
these lines: 'The country is going to the dogs. The
government is getting bigger, stupider, and fatter every
day. We are getting taxed to death. People don't have
a sense of workmanship any more. The Protestant ethic
is dead. Everyone wants to get on the dole. It just
can't go on like this forever. How much time do you
think we have?' Being a full-time prophet, I answer a
question with a question, a time honored prophetic response. 'How much time do we have?' To do what?

"Ultimately, the individual who asks the question has
something in mind, or more likely, a whole package of
ideas. The problem is, he has not sat down to think
about what he is really asking. . . .

"What the person is implying is that he thinks that his
capital, including his life style, will run out on him
before time does. . . .

"How much time do we have? To do what? How much time do we have? To meet what kind of crisis? How much time do we have? To meet a crisis period of what duration? How much time do we have? To spend how much capital once we think we know the answers?

"If someone told you, to the day, how much time "we" have, what would you do about it? Really and truly, what would you do differently? If the answer is "not much," then it really doesn't matter how much time we have as far as your budgeting is concerned. So the question is more of a curiosity than a piece of information in a program of crisis-evasion. Do you really want to know?

"If you really do want to know, then decide for yourself, once and for all, do you think it will be deflation (prices falling, so hold cash), inflation (prices rising, so hold precious metals), price controls (black market supplies, so hoard goods)? Do you think it will be a period of terrorism, or revolution, or intermitent breakdowns of the public utilities (water, power, garbage collection)? Will it be martial law? Will it be rationing? Will it be world war? What do you think the most likely scenario will be? Until you budget your time and capital in terms of one or more of these possible scenarios, you ultimately think it will be good times as usual.

"Have you spent a weekend looking for a piece of ground? When you do, you will have taken a preliminary step toward serious breakdown. You don't have to buy in panic now, but have you at least looked? Have you bought a copy of Les Scher's *Finding and Buying Your Place in the Country* (Collier, $7)? These are simple steps. Use this spring for enjoyment but seriously. Spend a weekend just snooping around. Pick up a rural local paper. So it costs you a weekend. So what? Don't assume that you will always have time to shop. It is time spent in advance planning that will keep you from gross mistakes. It's the assumption that you have unlimited time, mean-

ing an unlimited guarantee on your present comfortable
life style, that can cost you too much gold or too much
debt later on. If you're short on capital, you will
have to spend time. If you're short on time, then don't
begrudge the capital and the expensive mistakes."

SUMMARY AND CONCLUSION

Yes, I do think cities are an undesirable place to live
even today. With what I see on the horizon, they are
going to become increasingly less desirable. There is
a potential danger of nuclear attack, which could termi-
nate quickly any efforts to go to a retreat. With the
economic crisis that I think we are going to face, we
could see a time of violence and looting in the city.

At some point the "frog" must decide that it is time to
get out of the hot water - that is, to leave the city
and move to a small rural community. If this is a decision that is going to have to be made anyhow, the ad-
vantages are multitudinous of going ahead and making it
now, getting established, becoming part of a community,
and doing all of your learning while the learning is
easy, rather than under crisis situations. I realize
that we are talking about a significant change in most
people's lives. In giving this advice, which I have
weighed carefully, I am trying not to be optimistic or
pessimistic but realistic. Even if you decide that you
are "trapped" in the city, most of our subscribers are
in a position that they could begin to look for the right
town and the right piece of property, and buy it now
even if they couldn't move there and occupy it immediately. For those of you who for years have felt, "I've
got to do something about this retreat business", but
have never done anything, perhaps the reason has been
that you looked at commercial group retreats and isolated wilderness cabins and they didn't seem to fit. Maybe this new alternative might be the solution, and would
enable you to begin moving in this direction and still
feel peace about it.

15

THE FIVE SURVIVALS

Reprinted from MISL #158, December 1977

In the last issue I reported on the New Orleans conference. It was such a pleasure for me to be there and to
meet many of my old friends and subscribers. It was also
an honor to share the platform with such men as Senator
Jesse Helms, Senator Barry Goldwater and the Honorable
Owen Horwood, Finance Minister of South Africa.

The talk that I made began with a quick trip through the
three trends that I discussed in detail in MISL #128. I
pointed out that I am not the type of economist who depends on a crystal ball (they are usually wrong). Rather, if I can find three points of a trend, draw a
straight line through them and project this line into
the future, I feel that I can get a fair idea of what
the future will be like in that regard, assuming that
there is no tendency for that trend to reverse itself.
There are many trends that I could have analyzed, such
as the continual rising of taxes, the oil and energy
trends, the trend toward increased bureaucracy, the federal deficit trends, and so on. However, I limited my
talk to the three outlined below.

THREE TRENDS REVIEWED

The first trend deals with the amount of money spent in
our welfare give-away programs. In 1935 when the Social
Security and Welfare system went into effect, there was
1 beneficiary for every 143 workers. Today there is 1
beneficiary for every 1.9 workers, and if you include
government employees (like the 20,000 now in the new energy department) which economically don't produce any
goods and services, it is 1 to 1. Add to this the baby
boom of World War II. When all those children hit the
grade schools we built new ones, which are now empty.
When they hit the high schools we built new ones, and
they are now empty. About the year 2000 to 2005, these
people are all going to retire *en masse*. At that point
in time we probably are going to have at least 2 or 3
beneficiaries per worker. At some point along that line,
the system has to break down. The workers simply cannot support that many freeloaders, and so we are coming
to a crisis there.

The second trend deals with interest payments. When I
was a boy, my father and my grandfather had this philosophy: Owe no man anything; if you can't pay cash, don't
go. There was very little private borrowing. Our government was not corrupt at that point, and so there was very
little deficit spending. Therefore, in 1935 the interest
payments were a very tiny percent of the GNP. Today in
the U.S. interest payments on public and private debt are
approximately 40% of the GNP. When we extrapolate that
line out, and you know how compound interest goes, what
happens when interest payments become 50%, 60%, 70%, 80%,
90% of the GNP? There is a breaking point at which the
interest payments can no longer be supported.

The third trend is the downtrend of the U.S. dollar. You
are all familar with the price escalation that we are going through. A few years ago - say 10 years ago - bread
was $.12 a loaf and a paper dollar or a silver dollar
would buy 8 loaves of bread. Today bread is about $.60
a loaf. But a silver dollar will still buy 8 loaves of

bread, because a silver dollar today costs about 4 or 5 paper dollars. The ratio between silver and bread has not changed. Paper money has just become that much worthless. As I extrapolate that out, I see that eventually paper money will become completely worthless.

CONSEQUENCES OF THESE TRENDS

All of these trends seem to be approaching a critical point somewhere between now and the year 2000. I don't know when the exact breakdown is going to be. I don't think that anyone does. But let us consider what will happen when they do break down. What is likely to happen in real terms when the workers can no longer support the freeloaders? I believe that at some point the government is going to have to decide to freeze the payments that they are giving to the freeloaders, in spite of the fact that prices will be continually increasing. If that is done, I think that it will only last for a few months. The time will come when the check that the welfare recipients get from the government will barely buy their rent and food. Soon afterward it will only pay their rent, but will not buy their food. Then what happens? For three generations, the do-gooders have been telling the freeloaders that they have a right to be supported. When their check will not buy the things that they think they have a right to, I believe that they will simply go in and take those things from the stores.

What happens when the interest payments become unbearable? Governments in all past history who have encountered this problem have normally repudiated the debt. This means that all bonds, among other things, would be cancelled, because the interest payments would break the back of the economy. Four-fifths of the volume of Wall Street is bonds, and only one-fifth is stocks. If bonds were all cancelled, Wall Street would be out of business. Were that to happen, either the U.S. government would subsidize it or come in and actually run it.

What happens when the paper money becomes worthless? It is likely that people would just stop going to work. Who is going to want to work for worthless paper? If the firemen, the telephone company employees, utility company employees, gas station operators, and mailmen all stopped going to work, we would have a breakdown of services.

I believe that many of the forces have been set into motion that will cause an economic crisis of gigantic proportions sometime between now and the year 2000.

There are many other things that could create a crisis, such as a Mideast war, an oil embargo, substantially higher oil prices, or a military confrontation with Russia. If one of these other crises doesn't get us, the economic one will. What I am interested in is helping you survive a major crisis and come out on the other side in good shape.

THE FIVE SURVIVALS

I would like to talk about surviving a coming crisis in five major areas. These are:

1. Physical Survival
2. Financial Survival
3. Social Survival
4. Libertal Survival
5. Spiritual Survival

There are many other types of survival we could talk about, such as emotional and psychological survival, but these have been included under spiritual survival. Let's examine these one at a time.

PHYSICAL SURVIVAL

None of the rest of the survival considerations will mean very much unless you survive physically. Some of the calamities that you might need to prepare for could include nuclear war, earthquakes, rioting in the streets, and severe food shortages. Many of the preparations that we have discussed in previous issues are valid with regard to all of these calamities. Every home should have a water storage program, even if you live on a farm or ranch. A friend of mine who has a nice sized ranch near here gets his water from a well. The electricity was off for a couple of days, and hence he was without water. We, too, had a minor calamity and had to haul water out of the creek in buckets, even though our house is spring fed. In Pasadena we had about 150 gallons of water stored, but didn't feel that we needed to store water when we moved to the ranch. How wrong we were! Believe me - we have now reinstituted a water storage program.

Second in importance is to have a food storage program. The ideal in my mind is to have about three months' supply of regular canned food, which you could continually use and replace on a rotating basis, and about one to two years supply of dehydrated food.

In addition to these two major areas, there needs to be preparation in the area of energy. That is, you need to be able to heat and cook and have light without the benefit of the utility services. This can be done with fireplaces, wood stoves, propane camping stoves, kerosene lamps, oil lamps, candles, flashlights and even your own small electrical generator. Also in the energy area, I believe that it is advisable to have extra gasoline stored. The ideal is to have a 500-gallon tank, which you use to supply your regular gasoline needs, and to have it filled monthly.

If you have not yet made the physical preparations to survive a crisis, I would recommend that you contact this company:

> Survival, Inc.
> 24206 Crenshaw Blvd.
> Torrance, CA 90505

This is a nationwide mail order service that handles dehydrated and freeze-dried food, and all other survival equipment that you will need. I personally know the owner, Bill Pier, who is ethically above reproach. He is service-oriented and has a genuine desire to help people.

FINANCIAL SURVIVAL

Along with the economic crisis there is also a banking crisis coming. I continue to predict this and I hope that you don't grow weary of hearing it. I would keep minimal amounts of money in checking and saving accounts. Right now, the major money to be made is in the commodities. Eventually, as the economic crisis gets nearer, we will want to be completely out of anything paper. This means that we will want to be completely invested in hard, tangible, usable things, such as gold coins, silver coins, land, cattle, tools and equipment. The primary store of one's liquid assets, at the time of crisis, should be in gold and silver coins. There should be one bag of silver coins for every member of your family.

However, let me hasten to add that if you move 100% into gold and silver coins today, you are taking an extremely defensive position and you are eliminating the posibility of profit between now and the economic and/or banking crisis.

SOCIAL SURVIVAL

The last situation in the world in which I would like to find myself would be in a cave, in which I had a year's supply of dehydrated food, several buckets of gold coins, sitting at the mouth of the cave with a shotgun daring anyone to come near me. That is not my idea of a fun way to live.

This then brings us to social survival. When the time of crisis hits, wherever you are going to be, you will want to have around you a group of friends that can work

together, help each other, and care for one another. By
the time the crisis hits, it is too late to start developing these kinds of relationships. Preparations for
social survival need to begin now.

Perhaps there is a group of families from your church,
service club, neighborhood or place of employment that
can become close. Once this close group has formed,
there are a number of things that can immediately be
done for the mutual benefit of all involved. The group
could form a non-profit corporation and buy their automobile insurance through this "co-op". They could also
buy food wholesale and sell it to the members in the co-
op at barely above wholesale prices. They could do a
similar thing with gasoline and many other items. It
may be that at some point in time, the group may want to
buy a piece of land and make preparations on the land so
that they could all drive their campers, minimotor homes
or trailers there during a time of crisis in the city.

Many of our subscribers are "superindependent". They
are used to calling all of the shots for their own lives.
To become part of a group means giving up some of these
individual rights. It has been this way since the beginning. If you want absolute and total independence, then
the cave is the only alternative (living in isolation).
However, I believe that what you gain by becoming part
of a group far outweighs the small amount of "rights"
that you have to give up.

LIBERTAL SURVIVAL

I needed a word that dealt with freedom and liberty and
could not find one, so I had to create the word "libertal". We could survive physically, financially and socially and yet wind up under a dictatatorship or some form
of government under which we had little, if any, individual freedom. That is not a very pleasant prospect. Fortunately or unfortunately, our libertal survival depends
completely on Washington, D.C.

244

Many of you wonderful but superindependent subscribers,
I believe, have felt that you would take care of yourselves when you saw America going down the tube. You
would not try to influence Washington, D.C. because you
felt that that mess on the bank of the Potomac was impossible to change. The reason I suspect that many of
you have felt this way is because this is how I felt until about a year ago. I would like to suggest that this
attitude of keeping hands off Washington, D.C. and trying
to stay an arms length away from it is the very course
that will cause us to lose our individual freedoms and
liberties. In order to have our freedoms survive, I believe that it is essential for us not only to get involved in the Washington, D.C. mess, but to take overt
and concentrated action to change it.

At the New Orleans conference, I asked for a show of
hands to see how many people during 1977 had written at
least two letters to each of their Senators and their Rep-
resentative in the House of Representatives. Very few
had written six letters, (that's only one letter every
other month!). I'd like to ask you that same question:
Have you written each of your representatives at least
two letters during 1977? If not, then I would like to
suggest that you are doing very little to help our collec-
tive libertal survival. How could your representatives
possibly vote on the issues in the way that you wish, if
they don't know how you think and feel?

I submit that we are in a war for freedom and that this
war is just as significant as the war was in 1776. However, the bullets of this war are letters, telegrams and
phone calls. Every time you fire off one of these to
Washington D.C., you are firing a modern day bullet in
this war to maintain our personal freedoms. I came back
to the U.S. to try to help salvage America. I hope that
everyone of our subscribers will be vocal and involved in
helping turn the U.S. government from its current policies, which I believe will spell the destruction of America as we know it, and with it our indivudual freedom and
liberty. Resolve now to be a super soldier in this bat-

tle for liberty during 1978.

SPIRITUAL SURVIVAL

I would hate to survive physically, financially, socially and libertally and come through it all bitter, angry at the world, disillusioned and sour. I pity the man who finds himself in that state. Instead we should be able to come through the crisis with peace inside and our hearts full of love and joy. This is what I call spiritual survival. And just as in the other areas of survival, there are also preparations that need to be made to survive spiritually.

Many people have written criticizing me for mentioning my religious beliefs. I in no way am trying to proselytize anyone. I do sincerely believe that the spiritual survival is by far the most important of the five survivals. If someone else can find true internal peace, love and joy in someway different than I have, praise the Lord! However, I can only share with you out of my own background and experience. Some people, for example, may make a lot of money buying copper mines. I have never had any experience in that area and therefore can only share with you how to make money in the areas in which I have had experience.

I tried many things to find an internal peace and none of them worked for me until about halfway through college, when I received Jesus Christ as my personal Savior. A tremendous change then occurred in my life and, among other things, the restlessness that I had felt inside disappeared and in its place was a beautiful peace. This peace continues even today and I am confidant that, regardless of what occurs in the future, the Lord will see me through with that peace enduring. Like Job, I could lose everything - family, houses, lands - and yet I would have an internal love, joy and peace because of my relationship to God the Father through Jesus Christ.

If you don't have an internal peace that is with you regardless of the current situation, and regardless of how the future looks, I would encourage you to seek such a peace. I am not telling you where to look for it; I am simply sharing with you where I have found it. My prayers are that each and every one of you will find and develop the spiritual strength that will be required for survival during the coming calamities.

SUMMARY AND CONCLUSION

The future is uncertain. Changes are rapidly occurring. Many major potential crises hang over our heads, such as nuclear war, Mideast war, or a banking crisis. If one of these major crises does not break, it seems almost inevitable that an economic crisis of major proportions will occur somewhere between now and the year 2000.

When any one of these crises hits, there could be rioting and looting in the cities, food shortages, water shortages, fuel shortages and so on. Preparations need to be made *now* to survive these crises. We have discussed the five major survivals:

1. Physical Survival
2. Financial Survival
3. Social Survival
4. Libertal Survival
5. Spiritual Survival

You might ask yourself this question: In which of these five areas am I the weakest? Whichever one that is, that would be the area to concentrate on first in making preparations. All five are important, but to me without any question, the spiritual survival is the most significant.

Three very wise men a long time ago spent a lot of time and money looking for Christ. When they found Him their quest had ended. I may not be as wise as them, but in a similar way when I found Christ my quest for peace had ended. I hope that you may have "peace in your heart and good will toward men."

APPENDICES

APPENDIX A

HOW YOU CAN BE PREPARED

by Jim McKeever

Now that you have read this thought-provoking book, why ot send copies to your loved ones? You could be doing hem a lifesaving favor by giving them a copy of this book.

If you would like to give away some copies, we could ail them directly to your friends, with a card saying hat the book is a gift from you, or we could send them ll to you to distribute personally.

- -

mega Publications
.O. Box 4130
edford, OR 97501

I am enclosing the amount shown below for additional opies of *HOW YOU CAN BE PREPARED*.

) _____ Copies of hardback at $14.95 each = $ _____

) _____ Copies of softback at $12.95 each = $ _____

lease add $.50 per book for postage and andling. $ _____

end these copies to: TOTAL $ _____

y Name _____

y Address _____

ity, State _____ Zip _____

ift to: _____

ddress _____

ity, State _____ Zip _____

ift to: _____

ddress _____

ity, State _____ Zip _____

ift to: _____

ddress _____

ity, State _____ Zip _____

APPENDIX B

McKEEVER'S
INDIVIDUAL STRATEGY LETTER

McKeever's MISL is an action-oriented newsletter with "how-to-do-it" information. It
is produced 20 times per year and contains
a main article by Mr. McKeever. His articles
deal with subjects such as Swiss banks, commodities, tax havens, inflation strategies,
new investment opportunities, physical survival, and many more critical topics which are
helpful to investors during these rapidly
changing times.

In each issue there is a section on gold and
silver, another on the stock market, a model
portfolio, and a summary of significant items
from other financial and intelligence newsletters.

In addition, Mr. McKeever gives his recommendations in key investment areas. His model portfolio for 1979 produced 132 percent profit.

Omega Publications
P.O. Box 4130
Medford, OR 97501

Please send me information about subscribing to McKeever's MISL.

Name _____ _____

Address _____

City, State _____ Zip _____ _____

APPENDIX C

MEET THE AUTHOR

Jim McKeever is an international consulting econono-
mist, lecturer, author, world traveler, and Bible
teacher. His financial consultations are utilized by
scores of individuals from all over the world who
seek his advice on investments, international affairs,
and physical survival. He has spoken at monetary,
gold and tax haven conferences in London, Zurich, and
Hong Kong, as well as all over the North American continent.

Mr. McKeever is the editor and major contributing
writer of *McKeever's Strategy Letter (MSL)*. He was
formerly editor of *Inflation Survival Letter*. In
addition to his extensive economic and financial background, he has "lived off the land" for a year on Catalina, hunting, fishing, raising his own food and building his own cabin. He is one of the few men who has an
in-depth knowledge and actual experience in both financial and physical survival.

For more than ten years he was with IBM, where he held several key management positions. With IBM, he consulted with top executives of many major corporations in America, helping them solve financial, control and information problems. He has received many awards from IBM, including the "Key Man Award." He is widely known in the computer field for his books and articles on management, management control and information sciences.

After leaving IBM, Mr. McKeever founded and was president of his own consulting firm. In addition to directing the activities of more than 100 employees, he personally gave consultation to the executives of client organizations. In this capacity, he was a consultant to, and provided computer processing for, such organizations as Campus Crusade for Christ, World Vision, Gospel Broadcasting Association, and Nicky Cruz Outreach. His counsel was sought by the executives of these and many other Christian organizations.

In 1972, Mr. McKeever sold his interest in this consulting firm and resigned as president in order to devote his "business" time to writing, speaking and consulting in the economic and survival field.

SERVICES OF THE AUTHOR

The various services and materials available from Mr. McKeever are shown in summary form on the reverse side. Please indicate your area of interest, remove this page and mail it to him.

Mr. McKeever would appreciate hearing any personal thoughts from you. If you wish to comment, write your remarks below on this reply form.

Comments:

Place
Stamp
Here

TO:

JIM McKEEVER
P. O. Box 4130
MEDFORD, OR 97501

- - - - - - - - - - - - - - - - - Fold Here - - - - - - - - - - - - - - - - -

NAME _____ PHONE _____

ADDRESS _____

CITY _____ STATE _____ ZIP _____

Dear Jim,   BO-701

Please send me the following:

[] _____ hardback copies of this book at $14.95
          each, plus $.50 for postage and handl-
          ing (check to Omega must be enclosed).
[] _____ softback copies of this book at $12.95
          each, plus $.50 for postage and handl-
          ing (check to Omega must be enclosed).
[] Information on your money management.
[] Information and other books by you.
[] Information on subscribing to your financial
    and survival newsletter, the *McKeever
    Strategy Letter (MSL)*.
[] Information on your speaking at a conference.
[] Please read the comments on the other side.

CUT HERE

CUT HERE